21
KESARIS

21 KESARIS

The Untold Story of the
BATTLE OF SARAGARHI

KIRAN NIRVAN

BLOOMSBURY

NEW DELHI • LONDON • OXFORD • NEW YORK • SYDNEY

BLOOMSBURY INDIA
Bloomsbury Publishing India Pvt. Ltd
Second Floor, LSC Building No. 4, DDA Complex, Pocket C – 6 & 7,
Vasant Kunj, New Delhi 110070

BLOOMSBURY, BLOOMSBURY INDIA and the Diana logo are trademarks of
Bloomsbury Publishing Plc

First published in India 2019
This export edition published 2021

ISBN: PB: 978-93-89000-40-5; eBook: 978-93-89000-41-2

2 4 6 8 10 9 7 5 3 1

Typeset in Adobe Garamond by Manipal Digital Systems
Printed and bound in India by Replika Press Pvt. Ltd.

Bloomsbury Publishing Plc makes every effort to ensure that the papers used in the
manufacture of our books are natural, recyclable products made from wood grown
in well-managed forests. Our manufacturing processes conform to the environmental
regulations of the country of origin.

To find out more about our authors and books visit www.bloomsbury.com
and sign up for our newsletters

This book is dedicated to the memory of all martyrs, the service of all veterans and the selfless conduct of all serving personnel of the Indian Army. We also dedicate this book to the unparalled bravery and exemplary courage of the officers and all ranks of 4 Sikh (erstwhile the 36th Sikhs).

Contents

Preface

In the humdrum of everyday life, where forgetfulness has become but a habitual phenomenon, it is not surprising to see history slip into oblivion. At a time when the 'present' is at war with the 'future', the 'past' fails to find its deserved place. Of course, many are familiar with the skeletal socio-political history of this nation, as is the purport of our school curriculum, but to know about battles and wars (besides the seminal victories or losses) is rare. However, it is important for a nation to appreciate her soldiers and for soldiers appreciate their legacy. To bridge the gap between a nation and the history of her armed forces, many tireless historians have given up their nights' sleep trying to retrace and retell the epic saga of battles and wars.

The Battle of Saragarhi is one such battle of which very little is known to the general populace. In this episode of our country's history, 21 gallant men faced the onslaught of 10,000 Orakzai and Afridi tribesmen on the fateful day of 12 September 1897. In a fierce stand that lasted for seven hours, these brave soldiers did not falter in the face of odds heavily stacked against them and laid down their lives to defend their post.

Reasons dictating the onset of wars and battles do not emerge overnight. There exists a bone of contention in most cases, if not all, and discontent often brews for years, sometimes decades or even centuries before erupting into war. Hence, even before the story of this great battle begins, it becomes undeniably essential to first understand the reasons that led to it. Another point to explain here is the fact that while this book may be judged as downright biased, such is the nature of this chronicle that a judgment cannot be entirely avoided. Having said that, we have done our best to base this narration on facts and recorded figures we have uncovered in the Army archives. While it was very hard to find information about these 21 soldiers of the 36th Sikh Regiment, now 4 Sikh, it was not impossible. *Ashes to Glory*, an informative book on the history of 4 Sikh, written by veteran of the unit Brigadier Kawaljit Singh, provided us with the basic framework for our research. The references to the socio-political landscape of the time in Colonel H.D. Hutchinson's literary work, *Tirah 1897–98*, were also helpful, as was Major Yates's work, *The Life of Lieutenant Colonel John Haughton*, which helped us paint an adequate picture of the Commanding Officer of the 36th Sikh Regiment during the battle of Saragarhi. These, and many other books describing the colonial era at the end of nineteenth century were required reading before we began writing this book. Of course, it would have been impossible to even start this book without the unremitting help provided by the Commanding Officer and officers of the 4 Sikh.

While we have tried to tell the story as simply as possible, and will make deliberate efforts to avoid a tone that resembles a history lecture, we as privileged legatees thriving on this country's rich history must pledge to carry this legacy forward before it is buried in the sands of time. Brief fictional episodes based on our assessment of the battle have been added before some chapters in Part II – we hope that these will help the reader connect with this piece of history at an emotional level. This battle deserves to be remembered, in isolation as well as a concrete testimony to the unparalleled bravery of Indians of which the world must be reminded from time to time. Therefore, everything that follows now will bear its own importance.

'*Waheguru ji ka khalsa, Waheguru ji ki fateh.*' (The Khalsa belongs to the Lord God! So the victory belongs to God!)

Part I

1

The Colonial Era:
A Backdrop

In the vicinity of the famous Golden Temple in Amritsar rests a little known cenotaph which bears immense significance in India's colonial history. Often overshadowed by the famed Jallianwala Bagh, this forgotten memorial is inscribed with a legendary saga at par with the famed battle of three hundred Spartans against Xerxes and his massive Persian army: that of a daring stand of 21 warriors against the mammoth onslaught of ten thousand enemy fighters that took place almost a century ago. The unprecedented bravery shown in the fierce battle forever changed the way Britain – and the world – looked at Indian soldiers, especially Sikh soldiers. However, unlike in the rest of the world where writers and poets have immortalized the exceptional valour of their countrymen in verse, Indian history books almost never mention the battle that once swept the British Parliament off its feet.

Taking a leap back to the nineteenth century will provide necessary insights into events that culminated in the epic battle that took place at Saragarhi, particularly those pertaining to the history of India, Britain, Russia and Afghanistan. Nineteenth century was a crucial period in the histories of these countries, one now known as the 'Great Game', derived from heightened tensions between Britain and Russia as they battled for control over important territories in central Asia. By the end of eighteenth century, even as India's wounds from the tyrannical rule of latter-day Mughal kings had not yet healed, it fell victim to Britain's desire for economic prosperity as well as recognition as a world power. After the French Revolution, European powers began to leave their shores in search of new lands to conquer, both for resources and dominion. In the early 1800s, the Industrial Revolution was beginning across the world and Great Britain was one such place where raw materials and new markets were in great demand in order to sustain the new industries. After Vasco da Gama landed on the shores of India in 1498, it was no longer hidden from the world that India was a country rich in resources and, for Britain, it became a priority to colonize India to stamp their authority across the world.

While Europeans were clever enough to use the idea of the 'white man's burden' to justify their colonization of other nations, it was these nations that would bear the brunt of Europe's burden during the Great Wars of the twentieth century, leading to a British victory that would otherwise have been impossible. In fact, even before the Great Wars, Indian soldiers proved to be invaluable in saving Britain from the humiliation of defeat in the battles fought as a part of the Tirah Campaign.

By the mid-eighteenth century, India had quickly become one of Britain's most important colonies as it was rich in tea, cotton, raw materials and labour. However, India was not alone in this exploitation for trade – it also included a nation important to the backstory of this book: Afghanistan.

Throughout the nineteenth century, the key players of major historical events that took place in and around Indian subcontinent and central Asia were Britain, Russia, Afghanistan and India. Not long after East India Company took control of India in 1757, British rulers of India started to fear that in the 'Great Game' Russia would launch an attack on India through Afghanistan and particularly through the North-West Frontier region (now Khyber Pakhtunkhwa in Pakistan). To counter this possibility, the British government decided to set up advanced posts in the region outside India's frontiers to keep a check on the potential threat from Russia as well as to promote British interests in central Asia. These advanced posts later became the battlefield upon which the heroic stand at Saragarhi was taken.

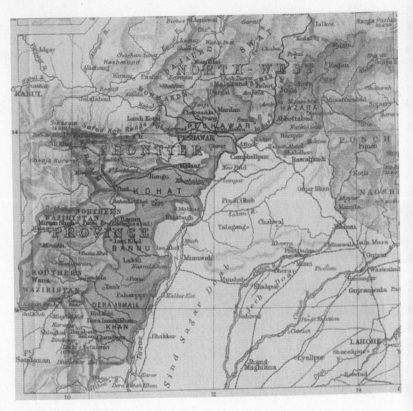

An old map of the North West Frontier Province

Both Britain and Russia were hungry for power in central Asia, but whose side did Afghanistan finally choose? In order to understand the answer to that question, it is important to delve into the country's own politics. In the 1830s, Afghan politics was going through an unstable phase under the rule of Dost Muhammad Khan. Despite his efforts to stabilize his territories, he could only succeed partially as his rule was plagued by a constant stream of threats, both internal and external. To the south, in Kandahar, one of Dost Muhammad's brothers was challenging his power and his rule. In the East, Maharaja Ranjit Singh, the legendary and powerful Sikh ruler of Punjab in nineteenth century, had extended his rule to Peshawar as a result of his ambitious campaigns; and in the West, Persia was rearing its threatening head. Dost Muhammad was trapped from all directions and with nowhere left to run, he chose to make an alliance with a powerful friend – Great Britain. While the Russians, too, tried to convince Dost Muhammad to join them, he was more inclined towards a British alliance.

While Dost Muhammad wanted to become an ally of the British Indian Government on the basis of complete equality and not as one of its puppets or subsidiary allies, much to his disappointment, he failed to get adequate terms from the British who would not offer anything more than verbal sympathy. As much as British touted the idea of the 'white man's burden', their agenda had always been to keep their colonies weak and divided, and that is what they planned to do in Afghanistan as well. After all, it would be easier for them to rule over a weak and divided Afghanistan. Hence, Lord George Eden, the Earl of Auckland and the then Governor General of India, only offered a coalition to Dost Muhammad based on a subsidiary system.

Having failed to make allies of the British India government, Dost Muhammad had to half-heartedly change his course towards Russia, who had extended their hand in support against the British.[1] These events, highlighting the quest of two hungry nations for power, eventually led to the First Afghan War in 1839–42 (which we shall only touch upon as briefly as possible). Lord Auckland, enraged by Afghanistan's alliance with Russia, decided to replace Dost Muhammad with a subordinate ruler Shah Shuja, who was deposed from Afghan throne in 1809 and had since been living in Ludhiana as a British pensioner. On 26 June 1838, a treaty was signed between the British India government, Maharaja Ranjit Singh and Shah Shuja according to which the British and Ranjit Singh would help Shah Shuja overthrow Dost Muhammad in return for the assurance that Shah would not make alliance with any foreign state without the consent of the British and Punjab governments. Following the treaty, the three allies launched an attack against Dost Muhammad's territories in Afghanistan in February 1839 and captured Kabul by August 1839 in what is known as the First Afghan War. The tables had quickly turned and Shah Shuja now sat on the Afghan throne as Britain's puppet. However, despised by the people of Afghanistan, Shah Shuja was overthrown as

---

1 Davies, Huw J., 'The Pursuit of Dost Mohammed Khan: Political, Social and Cultural Intelligence during the British Occupation of Afghanistan, 1839-4', London: King's College, April 2009.

a result of an uprising in 1841 that once again installed Dost Muhammad in the seat of power. Still licking her wounds, Britain organized a new expedition and reoccupied Kabul in September 1842. This time, however, it had learnt its lesson well; knowing that history could repeat itself, the British India government and Dost Muhammad arrived at a settlement on the basis of which the former evacuated Kabul and recognized Dost Muhammad as the independent ruler of Afghanistan. This tentative peace was predictably shattered after Dost Muhammad's death in 1863, and the tensions that had been simmering below the surface finally resulted in the battle that would immortalize the valour of a few brave men.

In 1885, the British India government and the then Emir of Afghanistan, Abdur Rahman Khan, decided to define spheres of British and Afghan influences and thus set up a boundary commission as a result of which the Durand Line – a 2,430 kilometres-long boundary line – was drawn up in 1893. The British India government, however, did not give up its 'Forward Policy'[2] and went on to occupy frontier lands inhabited by Pathans, setting

2 In the late nineteenth century, the British objective was not to set up a puppet government in Afghanistan but wanted Afghanistan to act as a buffer state in order to secure their occupied territories in India from Russian threats. Their 'Forward Policy' was in fact a policy of active vigilance against external threats, which included influencing events to suit the interest of security of the British dominion. The Durand line completed the chain of frontier settlements that began in 1872 and, in successive stages, gave Afghanistan a well-defined and stable frontier.

up military posts in the NWFP by drumming up the fear of a potential attack by Russia.

Having given an overview of the political scenario of the time, it is now time to complete the picture by acquainting with the people who came swarming into India in the thousands – fierce and hardened fighters who faced an unexpected challenge from merely twenty-one warriors, the heroes of this saga, the heroes of this book, the heroes of this country and its history.

2

Know Thy Enemy

The nineteenth century – one that had witnessed the nuances of the 'Great Game' – was barrelling towards its end. As explained in the previous chapter, relations between the British India government and Afghanistan were largely contentious due to the First Afghan War, followed by the disputed issue of Durand Line emerging as a consequence of Britain's 'Forward Policy'. Moreover, at the time, India was Britain's crown jewel and the British India government took an aggressive stance towards any perceived threat to India. After Britain's annexation of Punjab in 1849, it instated a 'closed border' policy that decentralized control over these border areas to prevent any outsiders from gaining access to India. It was believed that a friendly and independent Afghanistan would be a firm barrier against Russian expansion and their movement toward the Indian frontier, and the British decentralized control over border areas in return of assurance that Afghanistan would not build relations with Russia without British intervention. The latent threat of Russian imperial encroachment also led the British to recognize the tribal areas between Afghanistan and India as key territories.

However, this proved to be easier said than done. While Britain's policies allowed it to manage these tribal areas effectively, it lacked enough financial resources and forces needed to control the areas located in the difficult terrain bordering Afghanistan. Since they had occupied this land against the will of the tribes that lived there, they began to incur frequent raids into their territories conducted by angry tribesmen. These raids soon became a major pain for the British administration as these tribes were better acquainted with the tough mountainous terrain than the British forces, and raiding and looting was almost a way of life for them. As Colonel H.D. Hutchinson, an active participant in the Tirah Campaign of 1897, which was an Indian frontier war during 1897–98 in Tirah region to curb the uprising of Afghan tribesmen against British, who said, 'Bred and born amongst steep and rugged hills, and dark and dangerous ravines, inured to extremes of heat and cold, and accustomed from childhood to carry arms and to be on their guard against the wiles of the treacherous kinsmen by whom they are surrounded, it is small wonder that they are hardy, alert, self-reliant, and active, full of resource, keen as hawks, and cruel as leopards.'[1] As a consequence of their hostile behaviour, these tribes stimulated a bitter response in which British began to launch punitive expeditions in Waziristan in 1850s to punish the raiding Pashtun tribes.

Later in 1878, another Anglo-Afghan war took place, the details of which we would spare as of now. After this war, the British India government finally installed a permanent political administration in Waziristan in 1894–95. The demarcation of the state's boundary as defined by the Durand Line in 1895 added fuel to the already conflicted tribal areas when the Pashtuns refused to accept this new boundary as they believed that it infringed upon their independent status and separated them from their ethnic brethren in Afghanistan. This decade-long anger, pushed to the brink by the issue of Durand Line, finally erupted in a revolt against the British along the entire Indian-Afghan border in 1897. On 12 September 1897, 10,000 of these ferocious Pathans, a mix of two major Afghan tribes, attacked a British outpost in a place called Saragarhi, believing that there was an easy victory at hand.

Here, it is important to note who these people were, where they came from and what peculiar characteristics made them a potent and terrifying enemy.

---

1 Hutchinson, H.D., *The Campaign in Tirah 1897–98,* London: Macmillan and Co., 1898.

The Orakzai Pashtun Tribe

A group portrait of an Orakzai chief and three tribesmen, ca. 1900

There are numerous accounts that explain the origins of the Orakzai tribe but the most popular one states that in around tenth century AD, a Persian prince named Sikandar Shah came to be referred to as 'Wrakzai' or 'lost son' after he was exiled by his father for his mischievous deeds. Sikandar travelled eastwards and reached the town of Kohat, a city in the Khyber Pakhtunkhwa province in present day Pakistan, where he was appointed as a courtier to the king. When the king sent Sikandar Shah on an expedition to Tirah to punish tribals involved in looting travellers, he instead found a place for himself and settled there. As years passed by, he eventually became king. His descendants came to be known as Orakzais.

The Orakzais can be further categorized into eighteen main clans: Ali Khel, Uthman Khel, Feroz Khel, Zemasht, Sturi Khel, Abdul Aziz Khel, Daulatzai, Muhammad Khel, Lashkarzai, Massuzai, Alisherzai, Mulla Khel, Akhel and Ismalizai. The tribe was made up of both Shia and Sunni muslims, and the Orakzais also formed a part of the Mughal army; in fact, they are said to have established the state of Bhopal in India with the Nawabs of Bhopal belonging to the Orakzai ancestry. The British observers of the Orakzai tribe, in their many references and documents, express admiration for the fighting skills of this tribe but also condemn their bellicosity. British Colonel C.E. Callwell described them as 'marauding cut-throats', 'exceptionally fine mountaineers', admirable marksmen and 'ferocious adversaries'.[2] As per an estimate by the British India government, the tribe was made up of 28,000 fighting men. Not much is known about those who were recognized as the 'commanders' in this tribe, though, in typical tribal fashion the men probably

2 Johnson, Robert, *The Afghan Way of War: How and Why They Fight*, Oxford University Press, December 2011.

formed *lashkars* of five to fifty around a local influencer, a religious leader or a skilled planner. Many of these were well acquainted with weapons and mostly armed with the traditional *jezail*, the long rifled musket of the high hills around the tribal region.

The Orakzais were the reason for various British military expeditions to Waziristan, notably in 1855, 1868, 1869, 1891 and the Tirah Campaign of 1897.

The Afridi Tribe

Afridi warriors, ca. 1895

While the true origins of the Afridis are not clear, it is generally believed that Indian Buddhists of Aryan origin converted to Islam in the tenth century and formed the

Afridi tribe. Said to be the oldest among Pashtun/Pathan tribes, traces of Turkish, Mongol, Greek and other travelling tribes have been found in their ancestry due chiefly to their location on the Khyber Pass which, at the time, was a major east-west trading route. With an avid interest in trade, their tribe was also believed to be clever smugglers and this credit lies largely with the Adam Khel tribe of Afridis. As per the *Baburnama*, a treatise on the life of Babur, the first Mughal ruler to invade India, the emperor held a strong desire to bring the Afridis under his control mostly because they were a smart, daring tribe of well-built warriors. These tribesmen were exemplary in the use of weapons which they learned to yield very early in life. Unlike the Orakzai tribesmen, they were seemingly well behaved and some of them were surprisingly modest, but mostly superficially. Afridi tribesmen were stern followers of the Sunni sect of Islam.

Strategically, the geographical position of Afridi tribe was extremely advantageous. The Khyber Pass to the west of Peshawar, which gave access to the Kabul road, and the exit to Kohat towards the south, controlling the road from Waziristan to Baluchistan, was dominated by the Afridi tribe, which was why the British were interested in their territory. Afridis had eight important tribes under them namely Kuki Khel, Malik din Khel, Qambar Khel, Kamar Khel, Zakha Khel, Aka Khel, Sepah and Adam Khel, with their own ancestral villages in the Tirah valley extending down into Khyber Pass and Maidan.

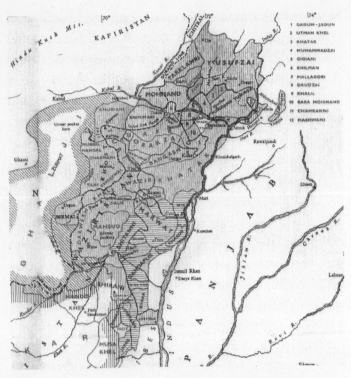

Map depicting the extent of the Afridi and the Orakzai along the 'Safed Koh' or the 'white mountains' in NWFP

Now that the geographical location and history of these tribes is clear, it is important to understand the characteristics of this potent and vicious enemy. Much has already been said about the warrior skills of the Pashtuns, but there also exists documented proof of the same. The Pashtuns, primarily a fighting race, were best suited to fight in their own hilly terrain. Their guerrilla tactics were legendary, and did from time to time baffle even the most organized of armies. In the nineteenth century, Colonel H.D. Hutchinson, a British officer well acquainted with the ways of Pashtuns, said that 'these men were extremely bold and they were cunning and clever as they were audacious. They showed much patience in watching and waiting for their prey and great dash and impudence in their attacks when they made them'[3]. This warring way of life percolated into their social behaviour as well. For instance, if a Pashtun man died of old age and not while fighting, it was considered shameful.

In Afghanistan, the Pashtuns were also cunning politicians and theologians. They purposed their lives with vengeance and believed in not leaving any business unfinished or any debt unpaid. Hence, family feuds were common among large families of the tribes. H.W. Bellew, a British medical officer, once remarked, 'The pride of a Pashtun is a marked feature of their national character. They eternally boast of their descent, their prowess in arms and their independence.' These Pashtuns were regarded by British officers as natural hill fighters who, they believed, could prove beneficial in Britain's army given adequate training and discipline. In one of the dispatches to *The Telegraph*, Winston Churchill, then a 22 year old young officer in the Tirah campaign, stated, 'Their swordsmanship, neglecting guards, concerns itself only with cuts and, careless of what injury they may

---

3 Hutchinson, H.D., *The Campaign in Tirah 1897–98,* London: Macmillan and Co., 1898.

receive, they devote themselves to the destruction of their opponents.'

However, even though Britain badly wanted the Pashtuns to be a part of their armies, they could not get them to agree, apart from few of them enlisting in border police, because these tribesmen felt nothing but hate for the British. By the end of nineteenth century, this hate erupted into a revolt against the British occupation of Pashtun lands as the tribesmen declared 'jihad' against British India, with more than 10,000 warriors rallying to the cause. Encroachment of tribal lands by the British in the mid-nineteenth century had sounded alarm bells among the Pashtun tribes who not only feared an invasion, but also felt that their way of life and independence would be destroyed by the British. The Pashtuns had always been sensitive about the occupation of their lands and, in the case of British encroachment, they strongly believed that the British government had deliberately and knowingly done so in order to dishonour and divide them. Decades after the annexation of Punjab by the British in 1849, extraction of land revenues from tribes caused anxiety among the tribesmen of the frontier region as they feared it was their turn after Punjab. As a part of the 'Forward Policy' employed by the British to build fortifications and roads in the vicinity of these tribal lands, the Pashtuns believed that it was only a matter of time before the British imposed their rule throughout the region and their tribes would be deprived of their ancestral rights to independently follow their culture.

This direct threat to their territorial integrity and cultural freedom is why the Pashtuns developed an aversion towards the British which, over the years, resulted in rallying and rising in revolt against the British forces deployed at the edge of these tribal areas. What is important to note at this juncture is that the British had mainly positioned their troops to thwart a possible attack by Russians or other ambitious nations. To do so, brave, responsible and time-tested Indian soldiers had been charged with this responsibility – Indians who the British knew were loyal to those to whom they promised their service. This loyalty would soon prove to be unmatched and unparalleled, as will become evident in the second part of the book.

3

Know Thy Battlefield

History is often prone to interpretation which, as a consequence of personal prejudice or as a deliberate attempt by people to influence others with their own version, can result in fluid narratives. It is therefore crucial to explain all aspects of a historical event so the correct conclusions can be made. With that in mind, let us know shed some light on another crucial aspect of this battle – the terrain.

Since the days when most of the world's most profitable trades were conducted via the Silk Route, Afghanistan has been strategically important, benefiting from the fact that it is home to a chief road providing access to all parts of central Asia. The same route that led to India provided trade opportunities to the British by connecting them to the Mediterranean Sea and Europe. Anything that passed through this route had to go through the tribal areas and, therefore, these strategically well-positioned tribes benefited by looting and raiding trading parties and British transport columns. This is one of the major reasons why the British executed their 'Forward Policy' and decided to take over the ancestral lands of the Pashtun tribes – The Kohat Pass.

The Silk Route

The Kohat Pass lies between the cities of Kohat and Peshawar on the Khigana mountain range in the North West Frontier Province of present-day Pakistan. The Kohat Pass led to Saragarhi, a border village on Samana mountain range, via Hangu. It was 50 kilometres from Peshawar, 52 kilometres from Kushalgarh, almost 100 kilometres from Tal and 135 kilometres from Bannu, a city towards the south of Kohat. The Kohat Pass was important to the British from both an economic and militaristic point of view. From the military's perspective, Kohat held importance as forces deployed ahead of Kohat in Fort Lockhart in the Samanarange, Fort Gulistan in the Sulaiman range – in Saragarhi, to be precise – could deny an enemy uninterrupted access to the pass and thwart any impending attacks from Central Asia. Commercially, the Kohat Pass was crucial in the trade of salt and other raw materials being sent to Kabul. Hence, the British came into an agreement with the tribes which allowed them to use the pass but they wanted a more permanent solution to the problem. When they decided to construct a road on the Kohat Pass in the year 1849–50, they began to face violent opposition from local tribes.

Ahead of the Kohat Pass lay the Samana mountain range, on top of which was situated Saragarhi, a small bordering village. The Samana range runs east to west, south of Khanki valley, marking the southern edge of the Tirah region. About 20 kilometres in length, its highest feature goes up to 6,000 feet. To its north lies the Khyber Pass. The Samana hills were captured by British in the year 1891 and fortified by building Fort Lockhart in the middle and Fort Gulistan towards the west. Rectangular in shape, these forts had stone walls that stood 15 feet tall with loop-holed bastions at each corner. Fort Lockhart had a holding capacity of about 300 men and Fort Gulistan could hold not more than 200 men. These two

24

forts were almost five kilometres apart, with an outpost called Saragarhi between them.

The caravan trade routes – a major reason for the British to divert their attention towards the outer edges of tribal hilly areas ahead of Kohat Pass – lay in and around the Khanki valley lining the Samana hills, in close vicinity to the north of Saragarhi. The valley was inhabited by the Orakzai tribe and, in terms of terrain, had nothing more to offer than rocky, rough mountains that were dust-coloured and tipped with snow on extremely cold winter days on its flanks. The mountain spurs gradually transformed into flat, plateau-like terraces with steep-sided ravines and a few streams and brooks rambling along the sides. The Khanki valley formed a part of the frontier strategically dear to British in the late nineteenth century.

Knowing the importance of this frontier, the British annexed Punjab in 1849 only to further its control in the bordering areas of the NWFP. After the annexation of Punjab, their first concern was to keep the pass closed for those looking to act against the crown. This was why the British formed a 'Three Fold Frontier' – the first being the outer edge of the directly administered territory of India; the second included the indirectly administered territory that was the tribal areas; and the third was the area demarcated by a linear boundary, i.e. the Durand Line. However, the British policies of levying taxes and fines, and sending punitive expeditions to suppress the tribes because of their interest in this geographical area is what gradually enraged the tribesmen and led to a battle where, in 1897, 10,000 Pashtuns declared war on the outpost of Saragarhi.

If we simply state that fighting in NWFP region was impossible without facing the fearful odds offered by extremities of climate and terrain, it wouldn't be enough. Understanding the difficulties offered by an unforgiving terrain, therefore, bears importance. As Colonel H.D. Hutchinson stated, 'It is to be noted that their country is like Caledonia, "stern and wild"; high mountains, precipitous cliffs, dangerous defiles, wild ravines and rushing torrents everywhere, while roads of any kind are conspicuous by their absence – a country therefore, in which strict "formations" and "precise manoeuvres" as we find them described and defined in our drill books, are impossible; and in which marches must be performed under conditions in which they become slow, exhausting processional movements, the long trailing flanks of which are dangerously exposed to attack from start to finish. The difficulties and dangers and risks involved in waging warfare against such a foe in such a country are obvious.'[1] To make matters worse, as understood from written accounts of officers who took part in operations in this terrain, the weather in the month of September of 1897 was not a very pleasant one. While sometimes the weather was bright

---

1 Hutchinson, H.D., *The Campaign in Tirah 1897-98,* London: Macmillan and Co., 1898.

and clear and one could see folds of rugged mountains edged against a dark blue sky, the high mountains offered nothing but the intense extremities of a cold climate. As an officer serving in the Indian Army who has served at far greater heights and in tougher terrains says, 'Terrain is the first enemy in every battle. Having experienced it for months, I understand the difficulties of cold, continuous precipitation leading to softening of mud creating cold muddy puddles everywhere, dense fog and reduced visibility, chill blains and frostbites, thinning of air at high altitudes and its effects on human body, especially on one not bred and born among such heights. Metabolism tends to slow down and fatigue creeps in even after a little physical work. But worse than the physical effects of such terrain on the human body are the psychological problems that surface from a monotonous routine and seclusion in a cut-off, distant place, leading to anxiety.'

On very cold winter nights, the temperature in the higher regions of the NWFP fell to as low as -5 degree Celcius and fierce winds would whip hard against the skin. A person unfamiliar with such terrain would have to be acclimatized which would then only aid in survival and not in overall physical efficiency. The Pashtuns, however, being born and bred in such terrain, knew it like the back of their hand, their bodies being better suited to this climate. Keeping this in mind, it becomes evident that other than the wrath of 10,000 strapping Pashtuns, our daring and mighty 21 had another problem to face with respect to terrain where their enemy, the light-footed master of the hill, was much better equipped than the 21 could ever have been.

Having dived deep into the socio-political situation of the nineteenth century along with the behavioural distinctiveness of the Pathans, while conducting a quick walkthrough of the tough and treacherous terrain, we must now proceed to the second part of the book where the story of a legend awaits – a historical saga so extraordinary that all exaggeration ever written in verse fades away in its light.

Part II

4

Guru's Kindred

It was the twelfth day of September in 1897. The morning sun crawled up the dark sky, returning colours to a waking earth. Golden rays streamed inside the fortress of Saragarhi, chasing away the chill from the night before, as dusty mountains sprinkled with snow peered over the fortress walls. On the eastern bastion, a saffron flag fluttered in the light morning breeze as 21 Sikhs made final adjustments to their beautiful turbans, buttoned the shirts of their *khaki* uniforms, the silver *karas* [bangles] on their wrists reflecting the light of the sun as they silently, one after another, walked outside to offer *ardaas* [prayer] in the presence of Guru Granth Sahib. Their voices echoed in unison as they sang verses in praise of their Guru's teachings, unaware of the fact that their voices would echo again later in the day as they shouted their battle cry, '*Jo bole so nihaal…sat sri akal!*'

~

The Battle of Saragarhi, made immortal by a clan of
'Khalsa' warriors, is one of the many testimonies to
the unequalled bravery of the Sikh race. The Khalsa
clan is defined by a strict moral code and well-defined
ethics, and their unsurpassed dedication and loyalty
has, from time to time, been immortalized in legends
and folklore.

To better understand the heroes of the Saragarhi
chronicle, it is now important to delve into the origin and
transformation of the Sikh race, as these core beliefs are
crucial to the stand they took that fateful day in 1897.
Quite simply, a 'Sikh' is one whose manners are plain and
simple, who is moderate in his conduct and honest in his
dealings with no dislikes and prejudices or superstitions
in his culture. Later transformed into a spectacular
combatant surnamed 'Singh' by Guru Gobind Singh, a
Sikh warrior was feared for his daring and revered for his
humility.

The Origins of the Sikhs

The history of the Sikhs spans the time of Guru Nanak,
the founder of Sikhism, up until the present day. It is
further divided chronologically into periods: from
the foundation of Sikhism to the establishment of the
'Khalsa Panth' by Guru Gobind Singh, from the rise
of Banda Bahadur, the disciple of Guru Gobind Singh
who conquered large tracts of land from the Mughals in

the 1700s, to the end of Maharaja Ranjit Singh's rule. The Sikhs originally and primarily hail from the state of Punjab, a region in north-west part of India, also commonly known as the land of five rivers where the inter-fluvial area between two rivers known as 'Doab' divides the state into the Bist Jalandhar Doab between the Beas and Sutlej rivers; Bari Doab between the Beas and Ravi rivers; Rachna Doab between the Ravi and Chenab rivers; and Chaj Doab between the Chenab and Jhelum rivers. The Punjab during British rule in India had larger expanse than it has today as it included the entire plain between the Jamuna and the Indus rivers. Its northern boundary extended until the Himalayas in the north and its southern boundary was marked by the desert of present day Rajasthan. Most of what is now Pakistan was earlier a part of Punjab, ruled by Maharaja Ranjit Singh in the nineteenth century before British annexation.

The region of Punjab has always held importance due to the fact that its abundance of river water and rich fertile land for cultivation coupled with moderate climatic conditions make this region most suitable for settlements. After Alexander's visit to this region, it was not hidden from the world that vast empires thrived in this region and it was not long before it attracted the attention of the Mughals. As a result, Timur, the recognized predecessor of the Mughal emperors, marched into India towards the end of the fourteenth century. Later, as the successor of Timur, Babur occupied Afghanistan with the intent of spreading his dominions in India. An ambitious Babur then led his Mughal forces and occupied the region of Punjab in the early 1520s. Following in the footprints of Babur, the Mughals would rule over the integral region of Punjab for over 200 years. During the time, the demography of this region was a mix of Baloch, Pathans, Gujjars, Brahmins, Rajputs and Jats. However, the Jats were larger than any other agricultural tribe and had gained numerical superiority by the end of the sixteenth century. During the Mughal rule in India, a variety of Islamic religious beliefs and practices were also introduced in the Punjab region. With this came a confusing mix of languages and dialects and, to this date, it is not clear as to which religion and what language was predominant in the region at the time.

In the midst of this religious, political and caste-based chaos, in April 1469[1], Guru Nanak Dev was born in a village called Rai Bhoi di Talwandi (present day Nankana Sahib in Pakistan). After his early education and marriage, Guru Nanak left his village in search of work, finally finding a way to make a living in the town of Sultanpur, which was then under the administration of Daulat Khan,

---

1 The date of birth of Guru Nanak has been widely debated for years. Traditionally, it is believed that Guru Nanak was born in the month of *Katik* (October-November) in 1469 which is why Sikhs all over the world celebrate Guru Nanak's birthday during that time. Modern scholars such as J.S. Grewal, however, have claimed that according to their research, he was born in the month of *Baisakh* (April) in 1469.

an important official of the Mughal empire. For a decade, Guru Nanak lived in Sultanpur with his family but neither his work nor his wife and two sons could keep his attention. He was displeased by the Islamic mysticism introduced into the region with its many superstitions and he began to search for the real purpose of human life, the true light of eternal knowledge.

Guru Nanak disapproved of the brutality with which the early Mughal rulers had begun to destroy temples and deplete religious freedom. Vedic education was being replaced by an interpretation of the *Quran,* and the message that there was no God but Allah and his messenger, the Prophet Muhammad, had begun to spread across the region. Guru Nanak believed that this weakening of the social order could not be saved by either Hindu or Muslim religious ideologies, and that a new set of ideas was required which would become the basis of a new social order devoid of prejudice and superstition.

After years of meditation, his search ended in a moment of divine calling and he set out on a journey to spread his message, leaving Sultanpur around 1500 AD. In the beginning of the sixteenth century, Guru Nanak visited important towns and religious centres of both Hindus and Muslims to question and debate with leaders of various religions practiced in contemporary India and to learn everything he could about society, politics, the education system, caste-based dealings, regional diversity and nature. As he reached his late fifties, his message of redemption, his logical reasoning and spell-binding preaching had begun resonating, attracting loyal followers from all across the Indian subcontinent.

His teachings were based on his belief that all life was suffused with divine light and all creation in this universe was His creation. He who was shapeless, formless, timeless, faceless, casteless and dimensionless and sat at the center of the universe, created a balance. Caste distinctions and social differentiation did not resonate with Him. For Guru Nanak, God had no 'caste' and He never discriminated against anyone based on whether they were born into a high caste or a low caste. In one of his verses, Guru Nanak says, 'Be there the lowest among the low, or even the lower, Nanak is with them.' Under the prevailing Mughal rule, the roles of Brahmins and Khatris were no longer relevant or well-defined, as a result of which their conduct degraded. The region, as Guru Nanak believed, was full of wrongdoers subsisting on the rightful earnings of others. He preached that those who followed the true path of knowledge were the true Brahmans and those who fought against the wrongdoings were the true Khatris: '*Satguru Nanak pargateya, miti dhund jag chaanan hoya.* [With the emergence of the true Guru Nanak, the true teacher, the mist cleared and the light of knowledge scattered all around.]'

Guru Nanak passed *sikhya* [instruction] to all who visited Kartarpur, a town on the banks of the river Ravi where he had finally settled for nearly a decade and a half before passing away on 22 September 1539. While the followers he gathered on his journeys cannot be estimated correctly, it is believed that most of his followers were from the state of Punjab. These followers who lived by the *sikhya* of Guru Nanak came to be known as Sikhs, a Sanskrit word for disciple.

With a core belief in the concept of equality and in the universality of spiritual opportunity, the ideas of Sikhism began to spread rapidly across the region of Punjab. It alarmed the Mughal emperors as the idea threatened their orthodox beliefs and soon the Sikhs were being forced to renounce their religion and convert to Islam. Sensing the looming threat against the ideals of Sikhism, the successors of Guru Nanak began to transform Sikhs into people who could protect their core ideologies.

The Transformation of Sikhs

The Sikh soldiers at Saragarhi would not have been as history knows them if Sikhism had not gone through a transformation post its inception. This transformation tells us a lot about the overall qualities, characteristics and behavioural customs that the Sikh soldiers of the nineteenth century inherited from their ancestors.

Guru Nanak Dev was succeeded by Guru Angad Dev, a Khatri of the Trehan subcaste and a petty trader; Guru Amar Das, a Khatri of the Bhalla subcaste; Guru Ram Das, a Khatri of the Sodhi subcaste and a young hawker; and Guru Arjan Dev, son of Guru Ram Das. These four successors, all from the Khatri background, took the reins of Sikhism in their responsible hands and guided it until the beginning of the seventeenth century. Each of these four successors contributed to the ideology of Guru Nanak in their own distinct way, working within the institutional parameters set forth by him. During this time, Sikhism evolved in terms of numerical strength, composition and social infrastructure. This is also when the concept of the community kitchen – called the *langar* – was introduced. The followers of the Guru would gather in congregation in a place of worship called the gurudwara where they would sing songs in praise of the Guru and listen to *bani* – the Guru's teachings sung by minstrels appointed by him. This idea of 'brothers-in-faith' and 'friends-in-faith' became a source of shared camaraderie among the Sikhs. Between 1574–77, Guru Ram Das got a sacred tank built in the present day city of Amritsar, one that was meant to remove the impurity of the soul and heart from the bodies of those who took a bath in it. The area around the tank slowly grew into a bustling town which came to be known as Ramdaspur, or the town of Guru Ram Das.

The Sikh of the early 1600s became more and more conscious, humble, righteous and non-violent, owing to the teachings of the Guru. A Sikh made by Guru Nanak was a man who did not retaliate and left everything to God. However, even as Sikhism spread far and wide, it drew the ire of the Mughals who wanted to keep the sect's fame and faith in check. While the Guru's successors encouraged their followers to cultivate profound faith and trust in God, it became difficult to remain non-violent in the face of growing atrocities committed against them, particularly when Guru Arjan Dev was tortured and executed on 30 May 1606 by the Mughal emperor Jahangir's men after refusing to convert to Islam.

In fact, Mughal emperors such as Jahangir, Shah Jahan and Aurangzeb wreaked havoc in the lives of Sikhs during their reigns. A few years after the martyrdom of Guru Arjan, Jahangir ordered the imprisonment of Guru Hargobind, the sixth Guru, in the fort of Gwalior. Having sensed the dire need of Sikhs being able to defend themselves, Guru Hargobind had moved away from Guru Nanak's core belief in passivity and started the transformation of Sikhs in earnest. According to historians, Guru Hargobind yielded two swords on his person: one symbolizing his spiritual authority and the other his temporal power. He encouraged his followers to train in martial arts, and those tired of the injustice towards Sikhs did not need much persuasion. Guru Hargobind also added two new features to Ramdaspur: first, a high platform, which came to be known as the *'akal takht'* or 'the immortal throne' where the Guru held his court; and second, as a part of his defensive strategy, a newly constructed fort called Lohgarh. This alarmed Jahangir, who ordered the arrest of the Guru. Later, while justifying the reasons for his activities, Guru Hargobind was able to convince the emperor that he was not a threat and was left alone to continue practicing and spreading Sikhism for the rest of the emperor's reign. However, after Jahangir's death, Guru Hargobind knew that it was only a matter of time before the new emperor, Shah Jahan, would wage war against him. Therefore, he developed a protective force around himself and settled down in Kartarpur where he managed to successfully repel attacks by Mughal forces.

The Sikhs had learnt to defend themselves under the influence of Guru Hargobind, but their troubles had only begun. After Aurangzeb succeeded Shah Jahan, he adopted a much more aggressive political and religious policy and went on to persecute every religion that wasn't Islam. The new emperor had also set his sights on the successors of Guru Hargobind, namely Guru Har Rai, Guru Har Krishan, Guru Tegh Bahadur and Guru Gobind Singh, the tenth and last physical embodiment of the Guru. In one of his compositions, it is revealed that Guru Tegh Bahadur had begun to prepare himself and his people for the worst. In May 1675, a group of Kashmiri Pandits met Guru Tegh Bahadur in Makhowal where they informed the Guru about the saddening situation of growing religious persecution in the Kashmir valley by its Mughal governor. Having thought about the issue for a long time, Guru Tegh Bahadur came to the inevitable conclusion that even if he was required to martyr himself to uphold his beliefs in the face of Mughal oppression, he must do so. After nominating his young son Gobind Das as his successor, he journeyed to Delhi to meet the emperor. When Aurangzeb asked him to perform a miracle as proof of existence of his God, he stated that occult powers were not a proof of God's existence. As a consequence, he was asked to accept Islam but when he refused, he was put in a cage and starved, as the three worshippers who had accompanied him were tortured and then killed in front of him. The first one was Bhai Mati Das, who was sawn in half; the second was Bhai Sati Das, who was wrapped in cotton wool and burnt alive; and the third one was Bhai Dyal Das who was boiled alive in a cauldron of oil. As a true devotee of Guru Nanak and his teachings, Guru Tegh Bahadur did not falter and was eventually beheaded in Chandni Chowk in Delhi on 11 November 1675. The Guru gave up his life for Kashmiri Pandits, who he had not known before they had come to meet him and with whom he shared no kinship whatsoever.

The reign of Aurangzeb was not a cherished time for Sikhism. While many of other faiths faltered in the face of Mughal tyranny and converted to Islam, the Mughals failed to compel Sikhs to do so owing to their supreme faith. Sikhs began to accept all atrocities as the order (*hukam*) of God – a test of their faith. Targeting the Sikhs – something that had begun after the martyrdom of Guru Arjan Dev – continued till the reign of Ahmad Shah Abdali (from 1748–67) in genocides that became known as *ghallugharas*. These atrocities are also recorded in the chronicle Tarikh-I-Alamgiri, written by Muhammad Kazim in 1865[2]:

> Abdali's soldiers would be paid 5 Rupees (a sizeable amount at the time) for every enemy head brought in. Every horseman had loaded up all his horses with the plundered property, and atop of it rode the girl-captives and the slaves. The severed heads were tied up in rugs like bundles of grain and placed on the heads of the captives... Then the heads were stuck upon lances and taken to the gate of the chief minister for payment... It was an extraordinary display! Daily did this manner of slaughter and plundering proceed. And at night the shrieks of the women captives who were being raped, deafened the ears of the people... All those heads that had been cut off were built into pillars, and the captive men upon whose heads those bloody bundles had been brought in, were made to grind corn, and then their heads too were cut off. These things went on all the way to the city of Agra, nor was any part of the country spared.

In spite of the dire consequences, the Sikhs continued to defend their right to worship, which angered the Mughals even more. They plundered Sikh settlements

---

2 Basu, Dipak and Miroshnik, Victoria, *India as an Organization: Volume One*, Palgrave Macmillan, 2017; Singh, Iqbal, *The Quest for the Past*, Xlibis US, 2017.

and gathered them forcefully to make them witness beheadings of young men and children who refused to accept Islam. Besides using torture as a tool, the Mughals also often humiliated the Sikhs by raping family members in front of them. This was when the idea of arming the Sikhs to defend themselves as envisioned by Guru Tegh Bahadur began to be implemented with utmost urgency.

5

From Sikh to 'Khalsa'

As explained in the previous chapter, the rise of persecution of the Sikhs led to the rise of the Khalsa Panth. The Sikhs were introduced to swords by Guru Hargobind, but all Sikhs as one race needed a show of unified strength to fight the odds stacking up against them. Many other elements of society who were dissatisfied with the Mughals, including Pathans such as Painda Khan, joined Sikhism which soon began to emerge as a rallying point for discontented elements, and those who stood for justice. The supreme martyrdom of Guru Tegh Bahadur only paved the way for the final transformation of Sikhs into an armed force.

Guru Tegh Bahadur was succeeded by his young son Gobind Rai, born in Patna, who soon came to be revered as Guru Gobind. He received literary education and gained expertise in the use of arms at a very young age, inspiring other Sikhs to learn martial arts with the underlying aim of building a fighting force from amongst his kinsmen. He founded Anandpur Sahib, a town with better fortifications than Makhowal – his father's town – or Lohgarh, in the vicinity of the former. A philosopher, a poet and a king, Guru Gobind soon gained fame even among the Mughals, who even feared him and his force. A story that showcases this fact goes like this: once, Emperor Aurangzeb sent a Mughal force to infiltrate Anandpur in the dead of the night but on learning that the Guru had been awakened by the guards, the commander of the Mughal force, afraid of facing the Guru in battle, fled with his men.

After proving his prowess in various battles fought against the Mughals, on the day of Baisakhi in 1699, Guru Gobind gathered a large number of Sikhs at Anandpur where, to the astonishment of the entire congregation, the Guru raised his naked sword in the air demanded a head. Awestruck at this strange demand, nobody came forward until a Sikh from Lahore named Daya Ram, a Khatri by caste, stepped in front of the Guru with his head bowed and hands folded in supplication. The Guru then accompanied him inside a tent that had been set up. A few minutes later, Guru Gobind repeated his call and this time, Dharam Das, a Jat; Himmat Rai, a water carrier; Mohkam Chand, a washer-man; and Sahib Chand, a barber, came forward and one by one accompanied their guru inside the tent.

Before long, much to the surprise of the congregation, Guru Gobind emerged from the tent with the five Sikhs who had answered his call. They were now all clad in beautiful robes and wearing turbans just like the Guru's. Guru Gobind then announced that the five loyal Sikhs would henceforth be called the '*Panj Piyare* (Five Beloved Ones)', and proclaimed that all Sikhs would now be known as 'Khalsa', uniting them into a military brotherhood. Cries of '*Waheguru ji ka Khalsa, Waheguru ji ki Fateh*! (Khalsa was creation of God and God has been victorious in the creation of Khalsa)' soon rose triumphantly into the air. Guru Gobind introduced into the religion the chastening baptism by the double-edged sword which obliged the Sikh to keep the hair unshorn, to wear arms and to bear the epithet 'Singh' (for men) meaning 'lion' and 'Kaur' (for women) meaning 'princess' in their names. Any of the five Singhs could initiate others into this new order. These imperative measures introduced the principle of unity and equality in the Sikh race. As a contemporary writer puts it, the Khalsa stood distinguished from the rest of the world.

In order to adhere to the order of Khalsa, a Sikh had to adopt the five K's namely *kesh, kirpan, kara, kangha* and *kachhera*. To show distinction, unity and equality among the Sikhs, baptized Sikhs were not supposed to cut their hair (*kesh*) and had to wear a turban which, earlier, only Gurus were allowed to wear. A ceremonial sword (*kirpan*) hanging from a cotton shoulder strap would be worn by all Sikhs, showing readiness to protect the oppressed, and defend against any injustice and persecution.

A baptized Sikh would also wear a steel bracelet (*kara*), symbolizing strength and integrity. A small comb (*kangha*) would be paired with the *kesh*, representing order and cleanliness. Lastly, baptized Sikh would wear cotton boxer shorts (*kachhera*), denoting self-control and chastity as well as the abhorrence of adultery.

As a response to this new development and its success among the Sikhs, Mughal forces were mobilized against Guru Gobind Singh and a siege was laid to Anandpur Sahib in 1701, cutting off the fortress from all supply routes. A long blockade ensued which led to depletion of supplies in Anandpur. Eventually, the Mughals promised safe passage to Guru Gobind, who agreed to evacuate the fortress with his followers towards the end of 1704 against his better judgement. The Mughals however, broke their pact, and decided to attack Guru Gobind Singh's convoy while he was crossing a flooded stream near Ropar.

In the din and clatter of this sudden battle, the Guru's wife, Mata Sundri, and his mother, Mata Gujri, along with his two youngest sons, were separated from him while he and his two eldest sons managed to cross the stream and halted at a village called Chamkaur where he was attacked again. In the famous battle of Chamkaur, all those who had accompanied him and his two eldest sons gave their lives fighting. Meanwhile, Mata Sundri was escorted to Delhi by a devoted follower even as Mata Gujri and the Guru's two youngest sons were held captive by Wazir Khan, the Mughal ruler of Sarhind. A cruel

Wazir Khan put the brave young sons of the Guru to death when they refused to convert to Islam. Mata Gujri soon passed away in grief. Finally, on 7 October 1708, in the city of Nanded, the legendary founder of Khalsa Panth, the bravest of warriors and the wisest of kings, Guru Gobind Singh breathed his last.

A year later, Banda Singh Bahadur, a devoted follower of Guru Gobind Singh who had met the Guru while he was in Nanded and was commissioned by the Guru to lead the Sikhs against their oppressors, led an uprising with the support of the Guru's followers to honour his and his family's sacrifice. After gathering enough men and material for the revolt, by November 1709, Banda Singh Bahadur had led a daring attack on Sirhind where Guru Gobind's younger sons were martyred, killing thousands of their enemies and razing Sirhind to the ground. He then raised more forces and conquered the entire area between the rivers Sutlej and Yamuna, fighting and winning over Mughal forces. He also introduced a new coin and a seal in the name of Guru Nanak and Guru Gobind Singh. The Sikhs quickly regained their lost glory, becoming fearsome opponents of the Mughals. Alas, after several successful expeditions, Banda Singh Bahadur was finally besieged by Abdus Samad Khan in the fort of Gurdas Nangal near the present town of Gurdaspur. Ending a siege that lasted eight months, Banda Singh Bahadur and over seven hundred of his followers finally surrendered towards the end of 1715.

In March 1716, they were executed in Delhi. A few of his closest associates were beheaded in front of him with the hope that he might reveal his army's strategies and give up their collected assets but Banda Singh Bahadur did not budge. He was finally executed in June after three months of imprisonment by being tortured to death in the most brutal way possible by having the Mughals gouge out his eyes with daggers, cut off his hands and legs with hot rods and beheading him as he fell unconscious.

After Banda Singh Bahadur's martyrdom, there was no immediate leader who rose to unite the scattered Sikhs, who then formed confederations among themselves. Later, Ahmed Shah Abdali, an Afghan ruler with the support of nearly 40,000 Afghans, came to invade India in 1759. In November of 1764, Ahmed Shah marched up to the town of Ramdaspur (now Amritsar) with his Afghan warriors and attacked the partially reconstructed Harimandir Sahib (the present day Golden Temple) which he had demolished two years earlier. Only 30 men under the leadership of a Sikh named Gurbaksh Singh stood in defence of the holy shrine. In the words of historian Ratan Singh Bhangu, 'Bhai (brother) Gurbaksh Singh with garlands around his neck and a sword in his hand, dressed as a bridegroom with his men forming the marriage party, waited eagerly to court the bride – death.'[1] As the Afghan forces drew nearer, the Sikh soldiers attacked and an unequal fight ensued, with 30 men pitted against approximately 30,000

---

1   Bhangu, Ratan Singh, *Prachin Panth Prakash*, 1809–1841.

until all of them met a glorious death in the battlefield. As an eyewitness to this episode of heroism, Qazi Nur Muhammad, a raconteur in the invading party, wrote in his accounts that when Ahmed Shah reached Amritsar with his army, they were attacked by a few men bent upon spilling their blood and eventually sacrificed themselves in a dutiful devotion to their Guru. In fear of the probable threat posed by the Sikhs, Ahmed Shah ordered their mass executions when they started to interfere with his brutal policies and fought his oppression in Punjab, looting his treasures and freeing innocent women from the clutches of his men. They fought gallantly, adopted martial arts and guerrilla tactics taught to them by Guru Gobind Singh. The Sikhs continued to face the horrors of Afghan brutality; Abdali and his forces were able to execute close to 30,000 Sikhs in a mass genocide. The massacre of Sikhs by Afghans is what stuck in the subconscious of every Sikh, serving as a century-old reason to seek their revenge.

By the end of the eighteenth century, India was introduced to the British Empire which would rule the country for another century and a half. During the same time, Sikhs started to unite under the leadership of Ranjit Singh, son of the erstwhile ruler of Sukerchakia Misl in Punjab, Mahan Singh, who unified confederations of Sikhs into one empire, becoming a Maharaja with a well-armed cavalry and troops whose training was at par with British forces. There were 300 guns in his artillery and about 20,000 trained infantrymen in 21 battalions, with a large number of Punjabis among them. As stated by the Treaty of Amritsar, the British recognized Maharaja Ranjit Singh as the sole ruler of Punjab.

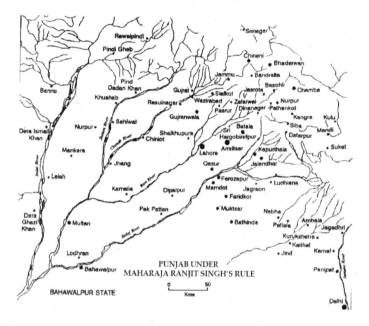

PUNJAB UNDER
MAHARAJA RANJIT SINGH'S RULE

The Sikh community, especially in Punjab, thrived in the early nineteenth century under his rule. He then led conquests in the former Mughal province of Lahore to expel Afghans from Multan and Kashmir and to, finally, take revenge from successors of Ahmed Shah Abdali for the years of persecution against the Sikhs. The state of Maharaja Ranjit Singh was soon stronger than many larger states in Asia. In the words of the Austrian Baron Charles Hugel, 'The state established by Ranjit Singh was "the most wonderful object in the whole world". Like a skilful architect the Maharaja raised a "majestic fabric" with the help of rather insignificant or unpromising fragments.'[2]

Before his death in 1839, Maharaja Ranjit Singh's authority spread over territories between the river Sutlej and the mountain ranges of Ladakh, Karakoram, Hindukush and Sulaiman, which was duly recognized by the authorities of Kabul as well as by the British. By 1849, this huge empire ruled in fragments by various successors after Maharaja Ranjit Singh's death was annexed by the British after these successors became pensioners of the British India government. The 'majestic fabric' that was woven together by Maharaja Ranjit Singh was now worn by Englishmen. Even employed under the British, a large number of Sikh warriors who now were a part of British Indian troops, remained a dependable force – a breed of time-tested fighters with inherent qualities of both followers and leaders. The simple, humble 'Sikh' created by Guru Nanak had survived over several centuries despite the almost insurmountable odds stacked against him and had forged his fate as Guru Gobind's envisioned combatant who would live and die to uphold the honour, traditions and beliefs of his community in the times to come.

---

2 Sharma, Radha and Bala, Renu, 'Society and Culture of the Punjab', Amritsar: Guru Nanak Dev University, 2011.

6

The 36th Sikhs

Havildar Ishar Singh, post commander at Saragarhi on the fateful day of 12 September 1897, fearlessly stood upon the bastion as he peered through his service binoculars while resting a leg on the parapet. The edge of his quoit, slantingly secured to his fortress turban, shone under a bright sun. A frown was gradually deepening on his forehead as he observed the swarms of armed Afghani tribesmen carefully sneaking up the hill from all directions. Slowly, as if foreseeing his fate on this day, he looked towards the sky with a gaze of acceptance and whispered '*Waheguru*'. He then went inside the fort to break the news of these developments to his subordinates, his companions, his brothers-in-arms.

'We will defend the post,' he declared. 'That is my decision and those who wish to leave, may leave now. Those who would accompany me, however – it is time for us to show these Afghans the valour that Guru ji passed on to all of us. It is time to avenge the massacre of our ancestors. They are not more than ten thousand in number, which is not even a fraction of what Guru ji expected us to fight against when he said, "It is when I make one Singh fight a hundred thousand that I am called Gobind Singh.'"

When a young soldier worriedly stated that they had been surrounded, Ishar Singh replied, 'They may have greater numbers, but we have greater courage. Yes, we are surrounded, but remember that only lions and falcons get caged, not crows and foxes – *"Kaava'n Giddraa'n nu kaun puchda hai, qaid sadaa hi baaz te sher hunde".*'

~

In almost two centuries preceding Britain's annexation of Punjab after the death of Maharaja Ranjit Singh, the Sikhs had made a significant mark in the history of the region. Moreover, their distinctiveness in terms of appearance, characteristics, high values and courage had been introduced to the British during the various Anglo-Sikh wars (1845–1849) fought as part of the annexation of Punjab. On learning of the vastness of Maharaja Ranjit Singh's territories and the fact that his well-trained forces comprised largely of Sikhs, it became almost necessary for the British administration to win the confidence of the Sikhs and induct them into their armies in order to exploit their prodigious skills. After the Sikhs – an entire race that was used to combat – were left with no reason to fight battles post annexation, they were convinced by the British to fight at the borders of Punjab in the vicinity of Afghan settlements, indirectly prompting them to carry out their ancestral vendetta towards the people of Afghanistan. Of course, it now becomes important for us to understand how the British were successfully able to recruit their former enemies for military service, making them their most fervent loyalists.

In the year 1857, when the East India Company was in control of administration in India, a revolt by Indian sepoys against British led to an uprising that swept across the nation. By this time, almost 3,00,000 Indian sepoys constituted the three presidency armies of Bombay, Madras and Bengal, against a much smaller British force. Several reasons could be attributed to this revolt including caste-based discrimination and grievance over issues relating to promotions, but the fuel to the fire was added by the British introducing the Enfield P-53 rifles to their arsenal. News spread among the Indian sepoys that the grease used on the cartridge of the rifle's ammunition – which had to be bitten before use – was made from cow fat, which was offensive to the Hindus, and pig fat, which was offensive to the Muslims. Under this 'religious frenzy' – as the British officials put it – the sepoys under their employ united and revolted across the nation.

In this turbulent time, a point of relief for the British was that, following their reconciliation, the Sikhs refused to join the Sepoy Mutiny of 1857. It was because Sikhs believed it to be treasonous to turn against someone to whom they had earlier promised their service. This unique moral code of conduct is why the British put their faith in Sikhs in the years to come, resulting in several battalions of Sikh forces being formed and thousands of turbaned and bearded Sikh men marching in the ranks of British armies. During this time, the British raised 18 new regiments consisting mostly of Sikh soldiers and making Punjab its armour against prevailing danger from outside forces. The history of the 36th Sikh Regiment can be traced back to this time.

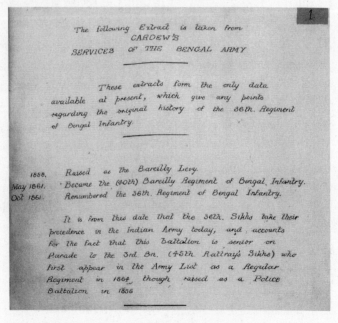

An extract from the first Digest of Service (1887-1913) detailing the initial raising of the 36th Sikhs.

Following the revolt of 1857, the administrative and military control of India was handed over to the British government by the East India Company according to the Government of India Act of 1858. The newly formed British India government began to consolidate all regiments and legions under the British Indian Army. Therefore, in 1858, the 36th regiment was first raised as the Bareilly Levy. The class composition of the regiment during this time is unclear. Later, in May 1861, the regiment was re-designated as the 40th Bareilly Regiment of the Bengal Infantry. In October 1861, it was renumbered as the 36th Regiment of Bengal Infantry. The 36th Sikhs take its precedence in the Indian Army from this date accounting for the fact that this battalion was raised before the 3rd battalion (which was called the 45th Rattray's Sikhs) that was created to be a police battalion in 1856 and who first appear in the army list as a regular regiment in 1864. Under the new Bengal Native Regiment of 1864, the class composition of the 36th was as follows:

(a) 2 Companies : Brahmins and Rajputs
(b) 1 Company   : Jats
(c) 2 Companies : Ahirs
(d) 2 Companies : Kurmis
(e) 1 Company   : All races and castes

Colours were granted to this regiment in the year 1876. In 1882, nearly 24 years after its raising, the British Indian Government decided to reduce some of the Bengal Infantry Regiments as a consequence of which the 36th regiment, along with 34th, 35th, 37th and 41st regiments, was among those chosen for reduction.

However, the regiments that underwent a reduction in 1882 were revived in 1887, including the 36th regiment as the British had to strengthen their armies due to the possibility of a Russian attack from the North West Frontier Province. They also needed more men to keep a check on the increasing tribal agitation in areas bordering Afghanistan. The 36th Sikhs of the Bengal Infantry was raised in Jalandhar by Lieutenant Colonel J. Cook vide Special Army Circular dated 23 March 1887 and a G.O.C.C[1] dated 20 April 1887. It was composed of a total of eight companies of Jat Sikhs of Punjab and a total of 225 all ranks or soldiers who were transferred to the regiment from the Bengal Army and the Punjab Frontier Force. The transferred ranks consisted of one Subedar, nine Jemadars, 25 Havildars, 26 Naiks and 164 Sepoys. The British also needed to recruit more soldiers, which is why a panel of British officers that included Lieutenant Colonel J. Cook, Major T.G. Thomson, Captain H.R.L. Holmes, Captain J.F. Worlledge, Lieutenant W.D. Gordon, Lieutenant C.E. Johnson and Lieutenant Erskine, led recruiting parties to the districts of Amritsar, Ferozepur, Gurdaspur, Hoshiarpur, Jalandhar, Lahore, Ludhiana, Nabha and Patiala from 1 May 1887 onwards. To recruit the best of the best, Captain Holmes, who was also a wrestler, followed a smart strategy in

---

1 *General Orders by Commander-in-Chief.*

which he challenged young and well-built Punjabis to a wrestling contest with a condition that those who would be worsted would have to enlist for recruitment. Tall, sturdy and masculine Sikhs accepted the challenge and this novel method stimulated more and more Sikhs showing up at the recruitment rallies. A total of 754 recruits enlisted between 1 May 1887 and 1 January 1888. Captain Holmes later retired in the year 1892. The number of recruits during this period inclusive of transferred sepoys totalled 816. The following officers were appointed to the regiment on 9 June 1887:

Commandant: Lieutenant Colonel J. Cook (Wing Commander of the 14th Sikh);

Wing Commanders: Major T.G. Thomson (Officiating Second-in-Command of the 25th Punjab Infantry), Captain H.R.L. Holmes (Wing Officer of the 45th Rattray's Sikhs);

Wing Officers: Captain J.F. Worlledge (Wing Officer of the 7th Bengal Infantry), Lieutenant W.D. Gordon (Officiating Wing Officer of the 3rd Sikh), Lieutenant H.L. Custance (Wing Officer of the 2nd Battalion), Lieutenant C.E. Johnson (Wing Officer of the 27th Punjab Infantry), Lieutenant C.T.A. Searle, Lieutenant C.E.H. Erskine;

Medical Officer: Surgeon G.H. Fink.

The first batch of officers of the 36th Sikhs

With the best recruits enlisted, a thorough training was required to turn these strapping Sikh men into efficient soldiers. Hence, under Cook's able command at Jalandhar, rigorous drills were conducted daily along with exercises in musketry and firing until 1891. The men surpassed all expectations, as is evident from the message of the then Commander-in-Chief of India, General Fred Roberts, written in the service digest of the unit after his first inspection of it on 10 February 1890:

> I saw the 36th Sikhs at Jullundur last November, and was much pleased with the setup and general appearance of the men. They are a splendid body, and the condition of the regiment reflects great credit on Colonel Cook and all concerned. In the Musketry

List the regiment now stands 8th. The fire control and discipline are said to be excellent, and great praise is given by Assistant Adjutant General for musketry, to the rapid, clear-cut section volleys delivered at emergency practice.

The 36th Sikhs remained in Jalandhar under training till 10 March 1891, after which the unit moved to Delhi where it stayed for a short duration and was then sent to Manipur in March 1891 to help curtail local disturbances and restore peace. This is where the regiment earned its first battle honour 'Manipur'. Later, after having successfully completed its duty, the regiment moved back to Delhi in September 1894.

The Sikh soldiers of 36th wore fortress turbans with a badge in the centre that was engraved with the letters 'XXXVI SIKHS' between two quoits atop which a crown rested with an embroidered border lining the badge. A fortress turban, usually bigger than the normal turban worn by Sikh warriors, offered a protective covering around the head with its cloth stretching for as long as twenty yards. A steel quoit, the signature weapon of the Khalsa, was secured to the turban for easy access during hand-to-hand combat. They also wore a scarlet coloured tunic with a broad patch of cloth in front. Overall, dressed in their ceremonial uniform, a soldier of the 36th was easily distinguishable from the other battalions in the British Indian Army.

An engraved insignia of the 36th Sikhs

After successfully conducting the responsible task of creating an efficient fighting force such as the 36th Sikhs, it was time for Lieutenant Colonel J. Cook to bid farewell to the regiment after seven arduous yet rewarding years. The first commanding officer of the regiment then relinquished his command on 25 June 1894. His farewell words as stated in the unit's service digest were:

> As the time approaches which concludes the term of my command of the 36th Sikhs, I feel impelled to place on record my sense of gratitude and keen appreciation of the cheerful assistance I have throughout received from the officers of the regiment and the ready obedience of all ranks, making the work a pleasure and a pride. The regiment being newly formed, coupled with the introduction of new drills from time to time, rendered the labours demanded more than ordinarily arduous.

I can only express a hope that labours so honestly bestowed may bring its own reward by the advancement of those concerned and the selection of the Corps for Service. In the course of my career, the period I look back on with most pride is that I spent with the 36th Sikhs. I need hardly add that I bid you all farewell, Officers, Native-officers, Non-commissioned officers and men, with the deepest regret at having to relinquish a connection with which I have been so intimately wrapt [*sic*] up for the past seven years. I shall watch the onward course of the Corps with keen interest and hope that if it be my lot to be further employed, it may be my great fortune to be associated with my old Regiment, which ever has my best wishes for its welfare in peace or war.

MAJOR-GENERAL J. COOK, C. B.,
Commandant, 1887-1891.

Major General J. Cook, the first Commanding Officer of 36th Sikhs

~

After Cook's departure in 1894, the command of the 36th Sikhs was taken over by Lieutenant Colonel John Haughton, an officer with less than 23 years of service. Prior to this he was a cognate appointment in one of the permanent wings of the 35th Sikhs, a regiment he had helped recruit for. A revered leader and a fine example of military traditions, history is replete with examples of his exemplary leadership and his competent command during the Tirah Campaign.

Lieutenant Colonel John Haughton

It is said that non-commissioned officers and troops constitute the basic skeleton of a regiment whereas adding flesh and skin to this skeleton is a commanding officer's job. The significance of a commanding officer in shaping the structure of troops and carving them into the finest possible soldiers with high morale and military values, therefore, cannot be ruled out at this juncture.

As stated before, there could be multiple reasons behind the choice of the 21 warriors of Saragarhi to stay behind and defend the fort on that fateful day in 1897, and one of these reasons could be their loyalty towards their commanding officer. In an attempt to understand why this could be so, it is important to brush upon certain traits of Lieutenant John Haughton that could explain the overwhelming interpersonal camaraderie that existed in that particular unit.

Haughton was born in August 1852 at Chota Nagpur in India to Lieutenant General John Colpoys Haughton who was at the time serving as an officer in the British Indian Army under the East India Company. After being educated in India until the age of 13 years, Haughton was sent to Britain for further schooling at Uppingham, where a memorial dedicated to him and his service as a soldier still exists. He entered the Royal Military Academy at Sandhurst when he was only 17 years old and passed out from there as an officer in the year 1871. In his book, *The Life of Lieutenant-Colonel John Haughton*, Major A.C. Yate meticulously describes his distinct qualities as an officer and a leader and what made his men regard and respect him. A detailed study of this book and other accounts of the officer from other sources paints a picture of a six-foot-six-inches-tall Haughton, who stood even taller in his stature. The reason that his men followed him in battle regardless of consequences was only because he was a leader who led from the front, as opposed to some other officers serving at the frontier during that time. In one of the letters Colonel C.H. Palmer wrote in 1899, he said about Haughton that,[2]

> How Jack [John Haughton] learnt to fight the frontier tribesmen I cannot tell you… [H]e was always reading useful accounts of campaigns, and I expect his father told him much of his experiences, and further, I think there is a sort of instinct in some men, as well as in mere animals, beyond the ordinary, or rather extra-ordinary human knowledge which makes one man 'all there' under certain circumstances, where another man of apparently equal mental caliber is an utter failure, and worse than useless, and I think Jack had this instinct; and further, Jack so thoroughly knew and studied the characters of all natives he came in contact with, and when you really know one native, or at any rate several of different castes and 'Jats' you can pretty well know what they will be likely to do in certain circumstances on service or otherwise.

It is said that war often reveals the truest character of a man, and at the time of the Tirah Campaign, Haughton's exemplary conduct and his humility and empathy towards Indian soldiers made him esteemed, respected and beloved. His qualities were not overlooked by his seniors and that is why, after steadily and sincerely

---

2 Yate, Major A.C., *The Life of Lieutenant-Colonel John Haughton*, London: John Murray, 1900.

carrying out his tasks for a few years, he was appointed as a commanding officer only after 23 years of service, considered young at the time.

It was from his letters sent back home from Samana Hills during the Tirah Campaign that we could place together pieces of his mindset and thoughts, as well as his worth as a son, a husband, a friend and a soldier. His manner and stance as the commanding officer of the regiment and his approach towards his men could be identified from the words of one of his dear friends, Colonel C.H. Palmer[3]:

> Haughton was kindly and courteous to everyone, but he would stand no nonsense, and could answer very curtly and brusquely to anyone who attempted to take any liberty with him. He had naturally a short and quick temper, but was so kind and tender-hearted that he would forgive and look over any fault or offence against himself, but he would do his duty in a matter of duty, however painful to himself.

Haughton married Margaretta Louisa Baker at St Bartholomew's church at Barrackpore on 18 January 1883. Unfortunately, his wife died in November 1884, just after the birth of their son named Henry Lawrence who, after his mother's death, was confined to the care of his maternal grandmother. In order to cope with

---

3 Ibid.

the grief of this loss, Haughton decided to devote all his time to his career in the army. He was appointed to carry out recruitment for the 35th Sikhs in 1887 and, by September 1887, the regiment had recruited a total of 912 soldiers across all ranks. It was during this time that the telegraphic news of the demise of his father reached Haughton. It left him with deep regret since Haughton had not met his father since he was 15 years old and had been eagerly planning to visit him. Nevertheless, he devoted himself to his service once again, as is expected from soldiers. In September 1894, he married Miss Helen Barmby at Durham, and assumed the command of the 36th Sikhs in 1894, an unusually rapid promotion that made Haughton an extraordinary commanding officer of a regiment destined to perform extraordinary service. Just before Christmas of 1896, the 36th Sikhs moved from Peshawar to Kohat and, in 1897, the regiment was ordered to take over the defence of Samana forts. Here, war with the Pathans put his capabilities to test and he emerged with the highest credit and honour to himself. On 2 September 1897, he was blessed with a daughter named Helen Katherine.

His dedication towards his regiment and his persistent efforts to develop a sense of camaraderie were a result of his own detailed study of the history of the Sikhs. He had also learned a Punjabi dialect to mingle with the Sikh men over the numerous meals he shared with his men in field. By the time he took command of the 36th Sikhs, he knew the Sikh soldiers thoroughly which helped his men to put their faith in him as their commanding officer. They fought valiantly with him in the Tirah Campaign and didn't leave his side even when their own lives were at stake.

An example of this is the battle that took place during this campaign on 29 January 1898. On that day, the 36th Sikhs was ordered to fall back for rest and to recoup after they had successfully driven away some Afridis, securing the heights of Kotal. However, Haughton, followed by another officer and handful of his men, decided to cross over the Kotal to help a neighbouring unit that was engaged in battle against numerically superior tribesmen. We will now let an officer's letter depict Haughton's courageous actions until he breathed his last[4]:

> He took a Lee-Metford rifle from a Yorkshireman, who was done up and kneeling down fired a few rounds to keep the Afridis off. About this time Turing was killed, and the few Sikhs with Haughton were either killed or wounded. He still held his ground to cover the retirement of the wounded. His hat was knocked off by a bullet, but he only said, 'That was a near shave', and turning to Major Barter, told him not to expose himself. Jack [Haughton] was absolutely fearless under fire, and would hardly ever condescend to take over. He then seems to have been left with very few men, for one of the survivors, a Yorkshireman, reported that Jack, seeing that there was very little

---

4 Ibid.

hope of successfully retiring, said, 'Now, my men, let us fire a few more shots, then charge the enemy and die like men.' He fired some five more rounds, and then fell dead with a bullet in his brain.

Lieutenant Colonel John Haughton was buried on 31 January 1898 with full military honours in a cemetery in Peshawar. A monument in his memory was erected over his grave by his fellow officers of the 35th and 36th Sikhs.

The true legacy of Lieutenant Colonel Haughton is described in an 1899 letter written by Major Dillon, an officer who had been in Tirah guarding the frontier: '...[H]is name had become a Talisman, and to many, as he was to myself, he was a dear personal friend. His name is still revered in his regiment, where he is talked about in the native ranks as something quite beyond the ordinary Sahib.'

This brief account of their commanding officer and the camaraderie that existed in their regiment throws light on the fact that the 21 soldiers of Saragarhi had trained and served under someone who had led from the front and fought with honour. Hence, this could have been one of the reasons they decided to defend the Saragarhi post at all costs – to stay faithful to the task bestowed upon them by their commanding officer who, they must have known, would have done the same if he were in their place.

7

The Twenty-One

Ram Singh lazily pulled the blanket up to his forehead, half asleep still, as morning sun rays fell on his face. Suddenly, the wooden door of Ram Singh's house burst open as a middle-aged man entered in a rush. An agitated Ram Singh got up from his bed, half reluctantly, and asked the man the purpose of his early morning visit.

'A telegraph has arrived in the district office. Your "*paltan*" [battalion] is moving to the Afghan border. You have been recalled,' the man spoke hurriedly, catching his breath after each sentence.

Ram Singh smiled. As a sepoy in the 36th Sikhs, he rushed inside to pack his wooden trunk, unaware that his mother stood in a corner watching. 'Why have you started packing? Your leave has just begun,' she asked, concerned, to which Ram Singh replied, 'O dear *bibi* [mother], we're finally going to the frontier to fight Afghans.'

Worried and equally confused, his mother asked him the reason behind his cheerfulness. 'Yes, I am happy, and why shouldn't I be? It is time for us to avenge the massacre of our ancestors and not everyone gets this opportunity that 'Waheguru' has now bestowed upon us. It is all His *hukam* [order].'

In a futile attempt to reason with her son, she asked why he was endangering his life for the sake of British interests. 'They gave me an *ohda* [position] in their *fauj* [army], *bibi*. Haughton Sahib believes in us Sikhs and treats us like his own. We eat and drink and fight together. We get food and clothes because they pay us. By staying behind, I cannot be the one to bite the hand that has fed me,' replied a motivated Ram Singh.

'We had finalized your marriage, son,' her mother said with regret, breaking the news to him. Ram Singh paused in his actions, his hand reached for his regimental uniform hung on a hook. Caressing the fabric affectionately, he said, 'A soldier is always married, *bibi*, and what better bride can there be for him than death in battle? Bless me so I do well, bless me so I do not falter, bless me and bid me farewell.'

His mother walked up to him, a drop of tear rolling down her cheek as she tenderly cupped her son's face with both hands. 'Blessed are the Guru's true sons,' she said. 'And you, my son, are one of them.'

~

A nation stands on the graves of her dead soldiers; their blood furrows her fertile green fields. Out of the brave 21 soldiers, many were young, not more than 30 years old since many of them were still sepoys who would have been recruited in 1887 or afterwards with the age requirement for recruitment at that time being 17 to 20 years. Similarly, with the help of information provided by 4 Sikh (erstwhile the 36th Sikhs) and visits to the Saragarhi memorials in Amritsar and Ferozepur, such inferences were made for all 21 soldiers before we stumbled upon a well-researched piece written by Gurinderpal Singh Josan, author, filmmaker and founder of the Saragarhi foundation, which helped us collate and write this chapter. Before delving into the events of the battle, we must first know who the 21 bravehearts were, so that they can take their well-deserved place in our memories.

Havildar Ishar Singh

In all of recorded history, one of the most consistent traits passed on from one generation to another is that we as humans have always needed a 'leader' to guide us as, inevitably, most of us are 'followers' by nature. Both are equally important but seldom interchangeable. In case of the military, a few characteristic qualities

No. 165 Havildar Ishar Singh

are necessary to make a good leader – namely courage, cooperation, stamina, determination, self-confidence, liveliness, effective intelligence, initiative, quick decision-making ability, social adaptability, the power of expression, the ability to inspire, reason, and organize, as well as a strong sense of responsibility. The soldiers at Saragarhi on 12 September 1897 were not short of a leader; rather, their leader was someone who was a fine example of a military man, with balanced qualities that had been forged in the heat of battle for most of his service. The 20 young men were led by non-commissioned officer Havildar Ishar Singh.

Born in the year 1858 in a village called Jhorarh near Jagraon, Punjab, Ishar Singh enrolled for service in the Punjab Frontier Force in 1876, and was later transferred to the 36th Sikhs in 1887. In the year 1893, he married Jiwani Kaur, little knowing that he would never see his wife again, since he left home a year after their marriage when his regiment moved to the North West Frontier to defend the border against Afghans. While Ishar Singh's soldierly conduct and his decisions on the battlefield were sound, and the orders passed on to him via heliograph (*see* Chapter 9) by his senior officers – who were witnessing the battle of Saragarhi from the other two forts in close proximity – were faithfully executed, he was hardly one to blindly follow his superiors. In the words of the British military historian Major General James Lunt, 'Ishar Singh was a somewhat turbulent character whose independent nature had brought him more than once into conflict with his military superiors. Thus, Ishar Singh, in camp – a nuisance, in the field – magnificent.'[1]

Ishar Singh, as we now know him, was a feisty and experienced soldier who sometimes preferred to march at the drum of his own beat, but was an exemplary soldier and inspiring leader. Such men, who cannot be fully tamed yet act within the restraints of righteousness, often change the course of history, immortalizing themselves and their deeds forever.

Naik Lal Singh

No. 332 Naik Lal Singh

Lal Singh, a 40-year-old naik at the time of the Battle of Saragarhi, was born in 1857 in Dhun, near Tarn Taran, Punjab. While there are no records that confirm this, it is likely that he was a part of the batch of soldiers transferred to the 36th Sikhs, taking into consideration his rank and age at the time of the battle, since fresh young recruits

---

1 Sohal, Jay Singh, The Saragarhi Foundation.

enlisted only in 1887. He was married to Bibi Prem Kaur, who died at the age of 57.

Lance Naik Chanda Singh

Chanda Singh was born in 1869 to Rattan Singh in village Sandhu, Patiala. Serving as a 28-year-old lance naik at the time of the battle, he must have been an excellent soldier to have earned a promotion at such a young age.

No. 546 Lance Naik Chanda Singh

Sepoy Ram Singh

Little or no information is available about Sepoy Ram Singh other than the fact that he was born to Sohan Singh in the year 1862. During the Battle of Saragarhi, this brave soldier was only 35 years old.

No. 163 Sepoy Ram Singh

Sepoy Sahib Singh

No. 182 Sepoy Sahib Singh

Born in the year 1860, Sahib Singh was a 37-year-old sepoy at the time of the Battle of Saragarhi.

Sepoy Ram Singh

No. 287 Sepoy Ram Singh

Sepoy Ram Singh was born in 1869 to Bhagwan Singh in the village of Sadopur in Haryana. A 28-year-old sepoy during in 1897, he must have been recruited between the ages of 17 to 19.

Sepoy Hira Singh

No. 359 Sepoy Hira Singh

Hira Singh was born in 1869 to Bara Singh in a village called Dulaowala in present day Lahore, Pakistan. He was married to Bibi Inder Kaur and had fathered a three-month-old daughter at the time of the battle. He was only 28 years old when he gave his life at Saragarhi.

Sepoy Uttam Singh

No. 492 Sepoy Uttam Singh

Uttam Singh was born in 1868 to Lehna Singh in Moga near Ferozepur, Punjab. He married at the age of 25 and at the time of Battle of Saragarhi, this fearless sepoy was only 29 years old.

Sepoy Daya Singh

Daya Singh was born in the year 1870 to Sangat Singh in the village of Khadaksinghwala, near Patiala, Punjab. At the time of the battle, this brave soldier was only 27 years old.

No. 687 Sepoy Daya Singh

Sepoy Jiwan Singh

Jiwan Singh was born in the year 1869 to Hira Singh in the village of Nakodar near Jalandhar, Punjab. He sacrificed his life when he was just 28 years old.

No. 760 Sepoy Jiwan Singh

Sepoy Bhola Singh

Bhola Singh was born in the year 1865 and was 32 years of age when he fought and died during the Battle of Saragarhi.

No. 791 Sepoy Bhola Singh

Signalman Gurmukh Singh

No. 1733 Signalman Gurmukh Singh

Gurmukh Singh was born in the year 1874 to Garja Singh in the village Kamana, Garhshanker in Punjab. Singh, a young signaller at the Saragarhi fort, played a very important role during the battle. It is because of his communication with the the unit in Fort Lockhart that information about the events as they happened was successfully relayed. If this soldier would not have done his duty well under the pressure of battle, most of the details we now know would have remained a mystery. In the later part of the book, when the battle is described in detail, his actions will be expanded upon further.

Sepoy Narain Singh

Narain Singh was born in 1867 to Gujjar Singh. During the Battle of Saragarhi, he was 30 years old.

No. 834 Sepoy Narain Singh

Sepoy Jiwan Singh

Jiwan Singh was born in 1869 to Noopa Singh. During the battle of Saragarhi, he was merely 28 years old.

No. 871 Sepoy Jiwan Singh

Sepoy Nand Singh

No. 1221 Sepoy Nand Singh

Nand Singh was born in 1873 in the village of Attowal near Hoshiarpur, Punjab. He gave his life at a mere 24 years of age.

Sepoy Bhagwan Singh

No. 1257 Sepoy Bhagwan Singh

Bhagwan Singh was born in 1872 to Hira Singh in a village near Amargarh, Patiala. During the battle of Saragarhi, he was only 25 years old.

Sepoy Bhagwan Singh

Bhagwan Singh was born in 1873 to Bir Singh. At the time of the battle, he was just 24 years old.

No. 1265 Sepoy Bhagwan Singh

Sepoy Sundar Singh

Sundar Singh was born in 1870 to Sudh Singh. At Saragarhi, he was 27 years old.

No. 1321 Sepoy Sundar Singh

Sepoy Buta Singh

No. 1556 Sepoy
Buta Singh

Buta Singh was born in 1868 to Charhat Singh and gave his life at just 29 years of age.

Sepoy Jiwan Singh

No. 1651 Sepoy
Jiwan Singh

Jiwan Singh was born in 1873 to Kirpa Singh. During the battle, he was only 24 years of age.

Sepoy Gurmukh Singh

Gurmukh Singh was born in 1870 to Rann Singh. He was 27 when he gave his life on the battlefield.

No. 814 Sepoy
Gurmukh Singh

NCE Camper Khuda Dadh

NCE Camper
Khuda Dadh

Though Saragarhi was defended by 21 combatants, there was one more man present there that fateful day in 1897 – the non-combatant NCE Camper Khuda Dadh, who laid down his life along with the Sikh soldiers in an effort to save the post of Saragarhi. During the attack on Saragarhi, he is said to have faithfully carried out his duty by helping the fighting troops in opening ammunition boxes and loading ammunition for the combatants, providing them with water and looking after the wounded, and who, having learnt how to fire a rifle in the hour of the need, fought a few tribesmen before laying down his life. Khuda Dadh was born in the year 1857 in Nowshehra (in present day Pakistan) and was only forty years old during the battle of Saragarhi.

~

It has been more than 100 years since the Battle of Saragarhi, but the sacrifice of these brave soldiers must not be forgotten. All of them gave their lives on the battlefield but not before they had already left a significant mark on the canvas of time, painting a picture of selfless service that would continue to be the guiding light to future generations of young men and women in uniform.

8

Tensions in Tirah

Outside, 10,000 Afridi and Orakzai Afghans marched, hungry for their old enemy's blood. Inside, 21 soldiers and a non-combatant Muslim, all briefed, motivated and led by Havildar Ishar Singh, stood ready to face them. The walls of Saragarhi were the only thing standing in between them both. A dead silence fell over the valley – silence born of anxiety and uncertainty. While numerically superior, the Afghans knew what the Sikhs were capable of and knew that number alone would not win them this battle. The 21 soldiers, meanwhile, stood fearless under the *kesari* (saffron) flag that fluttered over Saragarhi.

'I see a white flag,' said Sepoy Gurmukh Singh, turning to Havildar Ishar Singh. 'They want to talk'.

With a grin behind his thick beard, Ishar Singh replied, 'Then we shall let them talk.'

Ishar Singh climbed the parapet and saw the leader of the tribes advancing with a column of a few tribesmen and a flagbearer, who then halted at a safe distance. 'Don't you see, foolish Singh? We are in the thousands,' shouted a proud leader of the tribesmen. 'I admire your decision to stay and fight but you won't stand our onslaught for even a few minutes. So, I hereby offer you safe passage if you surrender.'

Ishar Singh glanced at his men and was pleased to see that they remained unaffected by the tribe leader's announcement and stood as firm as before. He then looked the leader in the eye and said, 'You *Jehadis* had once promised our Guru Gobind Singh safe passage and then betrayed him, and we are only a few ordinary men. Go and prepare your men for battle and pray that they do not falter when we roar. Today, you face the Guru's sons.'

For another moment silence prevailed, only to be broken by Ishar Singh who turned to his men and, quoting Bhagat Kabir, said, '*Gagan damama baajeyo, pariyo nisaane ghao, khet jo mandeyo soorma ab joojhan ko daau, soora so pehchaaniye jo ladey deen ke het, purja purja katt marey, kabahu na chhaadeh khet* (The sky echoes the sounds of the kettle-drum, the heart is pierced with passion for righteousness, the hero is engaged in battle, now is the time to fight unto the last. He alone is the hero who fights and defends the needy and helpless, who even though hacked from limb to limb; he will not flee the field).'

A charged up Gurmukh Singh then roared: '*Bole so nihaal!*' to which they all replied in unison: '*Sat sri akal!*' Their war cry echoed in the Samana valley for one last time.

~

The battle of Saragarhi was one of the many battles fought as part of the Tirah Campaign in which the 36th Sikhs played the important role of defending the forts at Samana hills. It is true that battle stress is a fine test of a soldier's character whose reputation, proportional to his actions in battle, is either made or lost. It is when a man is consciously aware of the fate that awaits him that he will unknowingly perform the most honest actions driven by his core characteristics. In the campaign of Tirah and in defence of the Samana forts, the reputation of 36th Sikhs and its 21 soldiers at Saragarhi soared to levels not expected by any at the time.

In India, 1897 was a turbulent year, with challenges to the British India government emerging from both the hinterland and the frontiers. Where many regions fought famine and plague, an uprising in the North West Frontier became the bane of the administration's existence. Tensions between the British and the Afghan tribes had escalated in the Tirah valley (that now lies between Pakistan and Afghanistan) to the extent that the British knew it could not be solved by dialogue between the warring groups. These tensions would eventually lead to many iconic battles fought by the natives of India along the frontiers, of which the Battle of Saragarhi was a part. Therefore, it is important to understand how these tensions began and how they shaped the history of the region.

Unrest in the Tirah Valley

The Campaign of Tirah was a response to the refusal of the Afridis and Orakzais to toe the lines drawn by the British with an aim to check damage to life and property being inflicted by them on the British convoys on India's frontier posts. In the North West Frontier, the Tirah valley was made up of the highlands that lie between the Khyber and the Kurram, south of Safed-Koh mountains, which can be approached via the Kohat Pass through Hangu. The Tirah was divided between the Afridis, who resided in the north, and Orakzais, who resided in the south, with minor watersheds flowing in from the Kurram valley providing it natural defence against any expedition from the east. Since 1849 when the British annexed the state of Punjab, the area under the frontier region also came under British radar, with them moving up to Samana, a hill range in Tirah, but not yet occupying the mainland of Tirah. The Samana range runs westwards from Hangu, 50 kilometres west of Kohat and was surrounded by the Khanki valley in the north and the Miranzai valley in the south. Towards the north of Samana lies the Khanki valley, the general terrain of which was already discussed in brief in preceding chapters. The vast mountain slopes – barren, brown and sterile – shape themselves gradually into terraced flats the sides of which are furrowed with gullies of many ravines and streams. In the Khanki valley of 1897, as recorded in writing by those who visited it, the villages were not merely a group of clustered houses but the houses were quite scattered, occupying vast lands bound by apricot and walnut trees, which turned scarlet and yellow at the onset of autumn, painting the valley in colourful strokes. After the trees shed their yellow leaves in late autumn, a brown sterility, a sort of copper hue again swept through the landscape. The open flat land, called the Tirah maidan, was blessed with cultivable soil owing to the many waterbodies that had outlets in the valley. The entire area, not more than 50 square kilometres, was effectively utilized for the cultivation of cereal grains and a special variety of rice. The Orakzais and Afridis, the two major Pashtun tribes that resided in Tirah, about whom much has already been said, were born and bred on this very landscape.

The rising tensions in the North West Frontier region in 1897 was the culmination of constant skirmishes between the British and the local tribes of the region. The first ever expedition against Adam Khel Afridis was led by then Field Marshal Sir Colin Campbell (who became the Commander-in-Chief of India [1857- 1860] during the sepoy mutiny and is known for defeating Tatya Tope in the Second Battle of Cawnpore) in 1850 when the Afridis started to interfere with British columns as they traded through the frontier. It was the first time when these tribesmen began to be viewed as potential enemies by the British. These tribesmen disliked the idea of being controlled by anyone but their self-appointed leaders and were difficult to restrain within social limits and discipline. In fact, when the British made attempts to do so by inducting the Pathans in their frontier forces, the Pathan troops often offered little or no resistance to tribesmen rising against the British and prioritized saving their own lives when given a chance by the tribesmen.[1] Things, however, finally came to a head with the signing of the Durand Line agreement in 1893 between Sir Henry Mortimer Durand and Amir Abdur Rahman Khan.

The Durand Line Agreement

Afghanistan was a country strategically located in Central Asia on which both the British and the Russians had eyes and both wanted its territory to be under their influence as a part of 'The Great Game'. Therefore, Afghanistan feared an invasion from both of them. However, the fear of a British invasion was far greater since Afghanistan had a demarcated boundary with Russia but no such specific boundary existed between Afghanistan and the British Indian territories. Both sides laid claim on certain areas, especially in the North West frontier, and wanted them to be under their respective influence. In order to settle this boundary issue with the British, Amir Abdur Rahman Khan asked for a British delegation to be sent to Kabul in 1888 but the British did not comply at first.

---

1 Hutchinson, H.D., *The Campaign in Tirah 1897-98*, London: Macmillan & Co., 1898.

Later, many attempts were made by the British to settle the issue but Khan used reasons to delay the matter. Finally, he had to bow to British pressure and once again ask the British India government to send a delegation to settle the border issue – they formed one headed by Sir Mortimer Durand, who was the then foreign secretary in the British India government. As much as he wanted to avoid this delimitation, Khan believed this settlement to be necessary, as is evident in his own writings: 'Having settled my boundaries with all my other neighbours, I thought it necessary to set out the boundaries between my country and India, so that the boundary line should be definitely marked out around my dominions, as a strong wall for protection.'[2]

Before inviting the British delegation to Kabul, Abdur Rahman Khan had asked the British government to send him a map with the proposed boundary lines clearly marked out, and to state up front which parts of frontier land they proposed to take under their influence and sphere. The government followed suit but Rahman Khan was not pleased with the map sent to him in which all the countries in Waziri, New Chaman, Chageh, Bulund Khel, Mohmand, Asmar, and Chitral, and other countries lying in between, were marked as belonging to India. To convey his displeasure to the British, he wrote to the Viceroy stating that if the British cut those dominions

---

2 Wahed Alikuzai, Hamid, *A Concise History of Afghanistan in 25 Volumes: Volume 14*, Trafford Publishing, 2013

out of his influence, they would be of no use to them either since the tribes that inhabited the region would not stop their plundering raids on British columns. He also believed that since the people of these dominions were of the same religion as him, he would be better suited to rule over them. Upon receiving no reaction on this, Amir invited a delegation to Kabul nevertheless, however reluctantly.

SIR MORTIMER DURAND
British Envoy to Cabul

A photograph of Amir Abdur Rahman Khan (1880), and a sketch of Sir Mortimer Durand

The delegation was well received and negotiations ended with the formulation of the Durand Line. An agreement between the two sides was signed on 12 November 1893 by Amir Abdur Rahman Khan and Henry Mortimer Durand, commonly known as the Durand Line

Agreement. In the words of Vartan Gregorian, 'In 1893, caught between Russian pressure, British intransigence, and his own unwillingness and unpreparedness to start a war with the Government in India, Abdur Rahman signed the Durand Agreement.'[3] The agreement stated:

> Whereas certain questions have arisen regarding the frontier of Afghanistan on the side of India, and whereas both His Highness the Amir and the Government of India are desirous of settling these questions by friendly understanding, and of fixing the limit of their respective sphere of influence, so that for the future there may no difference of opinion on the subject between the allied Governments, it is hereby agreed as follows:
>
> 1. The eastern and southern frontier of His Highness's dominions, from Wakhan to the Persian border, shall follow the line shown in the map attached to this agreement.
>
> 2. The Government of India will at no time exercise interference in the territories lying beyond this line on the side of Afghanistan, and His Highness the Amir will at no time exercise interference in the territories lying beyond this line on the side of India.
>
> 3. The British Government thus agrees to His Highness the Amir retaining Asmar and the valley above it, as far as Chanak. His Highness agrees, on the

---

3 Wahed Alikuzai, Hamid, *A Concise History of Afghanistan in 25 Volumes: Volume 14*, Trafford Publishing, 2013.

other hand, that he will at no time exercise interference in Swat, Bajaur, or Chitral, including the Arnawai or Bashgal valley. The British Government also agrees to leave to His Highness the Birmal tract as shown in the detailed map already given to His Highness, who relinquishes his claim to the rest of the Waziri country and Dawar. His Highness also relinquishes his claim to Chageh.

4.   The frontier line will hereafter be laid down in detail and demarcated, wherever this may be practicable and desirable, by joint British and Afghan commissions, whose object will be to arrive by mutual understanding at a boundary which shall adhere with the greatest possible exactness to the line shown in the map attached to this agreement, having due regard to the existing local rights of villages adjoining the frontier.

5.   With reference to the question of Chaman, the Amir withdraws his objection to the new British cantonment and concedes to the British Government the rights purchased by him in the Sirkai Tilerai water. At this part of the frontier the line will be drawn as follows:

From the crest of the Khwaja Amran range near the Psha Kotal, which remains in British territory, the line will run in such a direction as to leave Murgha Chaman and the Sharobo spring to Afghanistan, and to pass half-way between the New Chaman Fort and the Afghan outpost known locally as Lashkar Dand.

The line will then pass halfway between the railway station and the hill known as the Mian Baldak, and turning south-wards, will rejoin the Khwaja Amran range, leaving the Gwasha Post in British territory, and the road to Shorawak to the west and south of Gwasha in Afghanistan. The British Government will not exercise any interference within a mile of the road.

6. The above articles of agreement are regarded by the Government of India and His Highness the Amir of Afghanistan as a full and satisfactory settlement of all the principal differences of opinion which have arisen between them in regard to the frontier; and both the Government of India and His Highness the Amir undertake that any differences of detail, such as those which will have be considered hereafter by the officers appointed to demarcate the boundary line, shall be settled in a friendly spirit, so as to remove for the future as far as possible all causes of doubt and misunderstanding between the two Governments.

7. Being fully satisfied of His Highness's good will to the British Government, and wishing to see Afghanistan independent and strong, the Government of India will raise no objection to the purchase and import by His Highness of munitions of war, and they will themselves grant him some help in this respect. Further, in order to mark their sense of the friendly spirit in which His Highness the Amir has

entered into these negotiations, the Government of India undertake to increase by the sum of six lakhs of rupees a year the subsidy of twelve lakhs now granted to His Highness.

The Amir of Afghanistan and the British India government formed joint commissions in accordance with the agreement which demarcated the boundary line from Chitral to the Iranian border by setting up pillars only in the sections where both the sides agreed upon the Line. This boundary line came to be known as the Durand Line, which is also the present Pakistan-Afghanistan border.

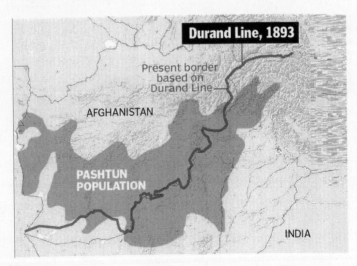

The Durand Line

The Uprising

The demarcation of a boundary between Afghanistan and India was not accepted in good faith by the tribesmen who lived in the frontier region from where the boundary was supposed to pass. Establishment of military posts by the British along the frontier added to the fear of the tribes who were already apprehensive about the idea of invasion. The Afridis and Orakzais revolted, stating that British encroachment upon their territory and interference with their tribal customs along with a hike in salt tax is what led them to revolt. Even to Rahman Khan, the idea of a boundary was distasteful at first. It took immense patience and countless negotiations before he allowed the British delegation to visit Kabul. None of the Afghans, including the Amir, wanted a change in their regime. Historians believe that the reason he agreed to sign the Durand agreement could be that he wanted the frontier tribes to act as a cushion between Afghanistan and India, with them now troubling India, so that his own territory remained secluded and safe from the reach of the British administration. The British also believed that the Amir spread the idea of *jihad* among all followers of Islam, stating that it was the duty of all Muslims to wage a war against the infidels.[4]

---

4 Hutchinson, H.D., *The Campaign in Tirah 1897-98*, London: Macmillan & Co., 1898.

Another reason for Muslims to follow his instructions or preaching was that the Amir had assumed the title of *Zia-ul-Millat wa ud-Din* which meant 'The Light of Union and Faith', calling himself the King of Islam, which was reason enough for blind followers of Islam to heed the Amir's words. Of course, these are assumptions are based on the reading of various books on the history of British-Afghan relations in the nineteenth century, and judgment must be left to individual discretion.

The study of this history also revealed that the Amir had maintained friendly relations with the British government. Upon receiving a letter from the British concerning his participation in the wars at Tirah, the Amir replied with a letter denying all or any responsibility in the tribal uprising. Furthermore, he repudiated all connections with the revolting tribesmen in a move to restore favour with the British government. His participation in inciting the tribesmen could still be true and is therefore left open for debate but, officially, he had no role to play once the revolt broke out. There also exists evidence pertaining to this fact. After carrying out the initial attacks on the Samana range in August 1897, the tribesmen requested the Amir for his support by sending a few important men of their tribes to deliver petition letters written by their *mullahs* dated 7 September 1897, the correctly interpreted purport of which is as follows[5]:

---

5 Ibid.

We have plundered and destroyed five posts on the Samana above Hangu... There are, however, three big forts on top of Samana (Fort Lockhart, Fort Saragarhi and Fort Gulistan) which have not been taken yet. By the grace of God we will destroy and burn these also. All the people of Tirah have taken up their position on the top of Samana; and at its base from Kohat to Rud-i-Kurman in the district of Kurram, the frontier of the Orakzai runs, and the tribesmen have been making *jihad* from time to time within their respective limits... We will never consent to tender our allegiance to the British government, and become their subjects. We will never give up the reins of authority of our country to the hands of the government. On the contrary, we are willing to tender our alliance to the King of Islam [Amir Abdur Rahman Khan]. It is incumbent on the Government of Islam not only to look after our interests, and consider our position, but that of the whole of Afghanistan... We are at present engaged in a *jihad* on Samana range, and we request that your Highness will be pleased to do what is for our good and benefit; and by the grace of God, we will act up to your Highness' instructions, because we leave the conduct and management of our affairs in the hands of your Highness in every respect... All the Muslims are now at the disposal of your Highness in the shape of regular troops, artillery, and money. If the British prove victorious, they will ruin the Muslims. The services to be done on this side may be left to us by your Highness. We hope that after the perusal of our petition your Highness will favour us with a reply.

These petitions, when carefully studied, display the edginess that must have gripped the tribesmen on realizing the gravity of the situation they had put themselves in, and that they alone would be unable to turn the tide in their favour, since the British government was not one to be underestimated, especially when it had the support and service of local soldiers at their disposal. Their initial attacks launched against British posts in Samana were enough for the tribesmen to know that their siege of the forts was not going to be carried out without heavy casualties. A bolt from the blue for them, however, came when the Amir sent his reply to the tribesmen on 23 September, turning down their appeal in order to avoid the wrath of the British. He, of course, stated various reasons in his attempt to appear just, as he also did not wish for the tribes to abandon him while he was in power. The same is evident in his reply[6]:

I have perused your petitions, all of which were with one object. I now write to you in reply that it is eighteen years since I came to Kabul, and you

---

6 Ibid.

know yourselves that I went to Rawal Pindi in April 1885 by the Khyber route. In consideration of my friendship with the British government I had gone to their country as their guest, and on my way I found many of your tribesmen on both sides of the Pass, who made *salaams* [salutes] to me. If what you state now is true, why did you not tell me at that time about the matter, so that I might have conferred with H E the Viceroy about it? Some years after this, when the boundary was being laid down, Sir Mortimer Durand passed through the Khyber and came to Kabul. All the frontier tribesmen knew of this, and saw the Mission with their own eyes. Why did not then your Mullahs, and Maliks, and Elders come to me when Sir Mortimer Durand came with authority to settle the boundary, so that I could have discussed the matter with him? At that time you all remained silent, and silence indicates consent. I do not know on what account now a breach has taken place between you and the English. But after you have fought with them, and displeased them, you inform me. I have entered into an alliance with the British government in regard to matters of State, and up to the present time no breach of the agreement has occurred from the side of the British, notwithstanding that they are Christians. We are Muslims and followers of the religion of the Prophet, and also of the four Khalifas of the Prophet. How can we then commit a breach of an agreement! [...] Therefore, on the day of the resurrection the first question will be about the observance of agreements. Infidels and Muslims will thus be distinguished by this test. You will thus see that the matter of the agreement is of great importance. I will never, without cause or occasion, swerve from an agreement, because the English, up to the present time, have in no way departed from the line of boundary laid down in the map they have agreed upon with me. Then why should I do so? To do so will be far from justice. I cannot, at the instance of a few interested people, bring ignominy on myself and my people. What you have done with your own hands you must now carry on your own backs. I have nothing to do with you. You are the best judge of your affairs. Now that you have got into trouble you want me to help you. You have allowed the time when matters might have been ameliorated to slip by. Now I cannot say or do anything...

Between the time the tribesmen made their request and the Amir's reply, the battle of Saragarhi had already taken place. Much had, by now, become evident to the tribesmen who had faced stiff resistance while fighting the British Indian Army. History had already been written in Samana and the ruins of Saragarhi continued to haunt the Pashtuns throughout the campaign of Tirah.

9

The Attack on the Samana Forts

The breach in the wall was almost complete and it was only a matter of time before it fell. Meanwhile, the fort's wooden gate, already riddled with rifle shots, went up in flames. Havildar Ishar Singh, who could see the horde of Afghans doubling their efforts now that entry into the fort was within reach, murmured, '*Waheguru meher karo* (God be with us),' not in fear or fright, but as a request to the Almighty to give him and his brothers in arms enough strength to fight the 10,000 now ready to pounce on them. Being an exemplary leader, he ordered the remaining soldiers to move inside the chambers while he stood in front of the weakened gate, ready to face the Pathans. However, after assessing the situation, the young Sepoy Jiwan Singh picked up his rifle and took position next to his leader. Another young Sepoy positioned himself next to Ishar Singh towards his left flank.

'I ordered you to move inside,' Ishar Sigh said with his gaze fixed at the door.

'No. We are staying by your side and fighting with you,' insisted the two soldiers.

'By staying, you will be defying my order for the first time,' Ishar said.

'...and the last time,' was Jiwan's stubborn answer.

Ishar Singh glanced at his men and nodded, knowing that they understood what they were facing. As the gate in front of them fell and wave after wave of bloodthirsty Pathans swarmed inside the Saragarhi post, the three men rushed forward to defend what was theirs until their last breath.

~

Now that we are familiar with the socio-political situation that led to the unrest in Tirah in the autumn of 1897, we can delve into the series of battles as they played out in the region at the time. The operations of the British Indian Army in Tirah, a wild and difficult stretch of land, tested the grit and proficiency of its soldiers (including those of the 36th Sikhs) more seriously than anything they had ever faced before. In fact, for most of the young soldiers, it constituted their first-ever field experience, a fact that made their heroics even more awe-inspiring. Post 1880, when the British built forts along the frontier and deployed troops to protect the passes and trade routes, primarily the Khyber and Kohat passes, the tribesmen who felt their territorial integrity had been breached, began to demand that forces should be withdrawn from Samana and Swat valleys. When their demand fell on deaf ears, the tribesmen, urged by their *mullahs*, began to assemble their fighting force with an aim to declare war on the imperial government, besiege their forts and close the Khyber Pass. The Orakzais and Afridis had the capability to muster a fighting strength of 40–50,000 provided all their factions fought together, but many of them chose to sit out the war. Their approximate fighting force, the one that participated in the Tirah revolt, is said to be around 20–25,000 men strong. Intelligence about the fighting numbers had reached the British government's military headquarters, but it came too late – the tribesmen attacked in the end of August 1897, and went on to capture and burn British outposts on the Khyber Ridge, Landi Kotal, Fort Maude and Ali Masjid between 23 and 25 August. In the face of this ruthless attack, the British Indian government had to respond, which they did by planning an expedition where a large number of troops were mobilized under the command of General William Lockhart, who had joined the British Indian Army as an officer in 1858 and was later made the Commander-in-Chief in 1898.

This was officially called the Tirah Expeditionary Force, and also included the 36th Sikhs.

After being moved back to Delhi from Manipur in 1894, the 36th Sikhs received orders to move to frontiers in the North West region. In November 1894, the unit marched to Ludhiana from Delhi on foot. In April 1895, after spending almost five months training in Ludhiana, the unit moved to Bannu via train, from where it left for Peshawar, arriving there in the same month. In December 1896, shortly before Christmas, the 36th Sikhs moved once again, this time from Peshawar to Kohat, from where it was sent to garrison the Samana forts. Before their departure, an inspection was carried out by Brigadier General E.R. Ellis to check the unit's readiness for the task ahead. His farewell order says it all:

> I am extremely sorry to lose such a fine regiment from my command. Since they have been at Peshawar, the conduct and soldier-like bearing of the regiment has been in every way excellent and I am well pleased with the regiment in every aspect. As long as we have regiments like this in the Native Army, we need never be afraid of anything. I hope they may soon have a chance of active service and I wish them every luck where they may be.

Defence of the Samana Forts

Fort Cavagnari

The 36th Sikhs's task was to start from Kohat and advance towards Tirah, taking up defences in the forts on the Samana ridge. Tirah, the summer home of the tribesmen, had never before been visited by the British. The 36th Sikhs occupied positions on the crest of Samana ridge at a height, strengthening its forts – namely, Fort Lockhart (or Fort Mastan) and Fort Cavagnari (or Fort Gulistan), 18 and 24 kilometres west of Hangu respectively. Both these forts were rectangular in shape and had walls made of stone which ran as high as 12 to 15 feet. In each fort, flank defence was provided by loopholed bastions at diagonally opposite corners. Fort Lockhart had the capacity to hold 300 men and Fort Cavagnari could hold almost 200. In addition, piquet posts, designed in the same fashion and similarly protected by loopholed bastions, were established at Saragarhi – a minor fort attached to a small village with largely Orakzai inhabitants – that lay in between Fort Lockhart and Fort Cavagnari, about three kilometres from former and about four kilometres from the latter.

View of Saragarhi from Fort Cavagnari

There existed other minor piquet posts as well between the two posts at Dhar, Sartop, Crag and Sangar. Each minor piquet could accommodate 25 to 40 men. Saragarhi, however, was held by 21 men and a non-combatant sweeper/helper. The fort of Saragarhi stood at a height of approximately 6,000 feet and was equipped with barracks for men, a guard room and a water storage facility. It derived its importance from its utility as a heliograph relay post (see next section) – since a direct line of sight was not available between Fort Lockhart and Fort Cavagnari, Saragarhi was set up to convey messages between the two bastions.

View of Fort Lockhart from Saragarhi

View of Orakzai country from the Saragarhi post

Heliograph Relay

Signalling has been an important aspect of war for years and signal equipment has been used by various armies to pass critical information, often changing the course of war. The torch telegraph was used by the Greeks, the Romans used coloured smoke as a means of passing signals and the English used beacons in the sixteenth century. For hundreds of years, long range communication relied primarily on individuals transporting messages and was only possible by using horsemen, ships, wagons, etc. This was until 1836, when a well-known painter and keen amateur inventor called Samuel Morse invented the Morse code – a character encoding scheme used in communication that encodes characters as sequences of two different signal durations called dots and dashes. Then came a device called a heliograph, which used Morse codes as light beams to pass information. To put it in plainer words, a heliograph is a device that uses flashes of sunlight reflected by a mirror to transmit signals. The beam of light falls on the mirror which can be interrupted using a shutter to produce flashes of varying length. Carl Friedrich Gauss, a German professor, is said to have come up with the idea of the device which could direct a controlled beam of sunlight to a distant station. However, the credit of developing the first widely accepted heliograph goes to Henry Christopher Mance of the British Government

Persian Gulf Telegraph Department who developed it in 1869 while he was posted in Karachi, then a part of British India.

The Mance Heliograph was a lightweight device weighing only about nine kilograms and required only one man to operate it effectively, as well as to carry it over distances. In one of the tests of this heliograph, the British Army was able to successfully send a signal over a distance of 55 kilometres, after which the device was inducted into the British Army's inventory and was first used in the Jowaki-Afridi expedition of 1877[1]. It soon became an important means of communication and was used for more than 60 years after its development.

The heliograph formed a mobile element in the British Signal units after having proven its worth in the field of communication during war. Using a heliograph allowed eight to sixteen words to be transmitted per minute, and the equipment was relatively cheap and easy to produce. However, one of the limitations of this device was that it could only be used in the presence of sunlight and not during night. Another factor that limited the use of heliograph as a means of communication was line of sight. A line of

---

1 In 1877, when British Indian government proposed reducing the allowance paid to the Jowaki Afridi tribe for guarding the Kohat Pass, the tribe cut the telegraph wire and raided the British territory, stimulating a response in which British military sorties were launched against them. A force of 1,500 troops penetrated the lands owned by the tribe in three columns, and did considerable damage by way of punishment.

sight clear from obstructions was necessary between the sender and receiver to receive light flashes, since we all are aware that light beams travel in a straight line. To overcome this limitation, relay posts began to be used. In this, a signal relay post was set up between two points not in line of sight but in line of sight with the relay post. The sender sent the message to the relay post, which recorded and transmitted the same message to the receiver, thereby acting as an intermediary repeater. The fort at Saragarhi, being a heliograph signal relay post, was equipped with the same task and thereby held importance for effective signal communication between Fort Lockhart and Fort Cavagnari.

Sikh Signallers with Captain Pratt. Heliographs and their tripods are placed in front.

Tactics of the Tribesmen

Before moving forward and discussing the initial attacks
on the forts at Samana, certain peculiar characteristics
about the warfare methods followed by the tribesmen
must be understood to answer the question – why did
the tribesmen not fight a conventional war with all their
strength concentrated in one place at one time?

The tribesmen, though clever fighters, believed in
sticking to their age-old tactics of mountain warfare.
They were dwellers of the hills who knew all defiles,
ravines, passes and boulders of Tirah like the back of their
hands and had discerned how to use the same to their
advantage. The very basis of their tactics was that they
were said to retreat as their foe advanced and then press
upon him as he retired. Their initial withdrawal gave a
sense of superiority to the advancing enemy even as the
tribesmen tactfully channelized them into a predefined
killing zone. Once inside this zone, the tribesmen
attacked their enemies with all their might. This time, as
the enemy withdrew, the Afghans attacked them from a
position of strength. If the enemy decided to press upon
them again, they withdrew again, thereby harassing the
enemy enough to cause panic among their ranks and
force them to commit mistakes.

Another particularity of their form of warfare was the
use of long range rapid firing breech loaders. In the revolt

of 1897, all the tribesmen were fairly well armed with the Martini-Henry rifle, besides their iconic 'Jezail'.

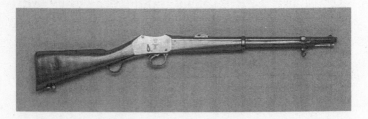

Martini-Henry Rifle, 1880

Rifles used in the 1880s: From the top, the 'Jezail',
the Lee-Metford and the Snider

These rifles were said to have been stolen from India by thugs who had sold them across the frontier to the Afghans. Some rifles were also stolen in the many raids conducted by the Pathans on British convoys. Along with the rifles, a huge stock of ammunition was also smuggled across the border, along with some explosives. They were also equipped with a quite a few Snider rifles, the weapon whose ammunition inflicted shattering wounds in the enemy, lowering their overall morale in battle. Hence, it is clear that, in terms of fire power, the tribesmen had the ability to hold their own against the British.

Arms and ammunition wasn't the only thing the British had to worry about. The tribesmen were also expert marksmen. An Afridi or an Orakzai offspring was introduced to arms at a very early age. Marksmanship was a qualitative requirement for them in order to be able to survive in their raiding tribes and feudal families. Ever since the British decided to induct Pathans in their border police and army, they had heavily enlisted in their regiments to the extent that at one time an entire company of Sappers and Miners was made of Afridis. Hence, when these soldiers retired, they rejoined their tribes with valuable experience that included knowledge of British battlefield tactics as well as their basic drills and battle procedures. This knowledge, when combined with knowledge of the terrain, made them a formidable enemy.

The tribesmen were natural mountaineers, and made the best possible use of this skill by attacking the

British transport columns from advantageous positions, knowing that these columns would march through defiles or river beds at the bottom of the valley. To counter this, British adopted a technique in which they marched in parties where each party had an advance guard and flank guards for protection. The flank guard parties were sent almost two kilometres in either direction to detect an attacking party at safe distances from the main body. Any surprise attack, therefore, gave them enough reaction time to either resist it or withdraw without suffering grave casualties. The tribesmen, however, were clever and would attack the enemy from a higher ground; when flank protection parties were sent in for a counter attack, they would withdraw back to the hills.

In the meantime, another group of tribesmen would attack the party from the rear. When flank protection parties who had earlier gone uphill would return to engage them, the hill attackers swooped down on them, thereby inflicting heavy casualties. They would quickly fall back in case the British advanced and only attacked when they retired. At times, they would appear all of a sudden to use the element of surprise in their favour. Another infamous tactic of the tribesmen was to shoot the enemy from behind a rock, then rush in with a sword to slay the survivors, finally retreating as swiftly as they had attacked, displaying caution as well as shrewdness.

The tribesmen were, therefore, smarter in the hills, not only while attacking, but while defending as well. Due to the difference in the geographical positions that the Orakzais and Afridis occupied in Tirah, both had adopted their own unique system of defence. The Orakzais sought refuge in the hillsides, particularly in caves that existed in the mountain wilderness. The Afridis, on the other hand, sought refuge in the valleys in the north, and considered the use of small passes or backdoors to retreat across the Safed Koh mountains if they feared an invasion at any time.

Under such circumstances, it became difficult for the British forces to follow their standard drills since it was a new terrain for them, as well as a new and fierce enemy. Such tactics of skirmish attacks by the tribesmen also prevented the British forces from reinforcing their other units. However, despite the losses, the British continued to move their transport columns through this region due to the lack of other viable options. Another annoyance caused by the tribesmen was that they denied the British the use of messengers to send communications across safe distances since the terrain was useless for horsemen and the messages had to be sent by foot which was decidedly unsafe. Moreover, the security of camps and garrisons was another major concern for the British. The tribesmen would attack the camps in the night, taking advantage of reduced visibility. They would hide in the cover offered by the terrain and use long range rifles to shoot at sentry posts or at patrolling guards with the sole purpose of wreaking havoc on the camp. Before the crack of dawn, they would retreat.

However, the British were resilient and it only required one serious blow to make them realize that they had had enough. This came in the form of the attack on the Samana forts.

The Samana Attack

The entire Samana ridge gained importance when the British built forts all along the ridge dominating the valleys on either side. To weaken the British, the tribesmen decided to attack the forts at Samana and capture them.

On 25 August 1897, the British government received information that a sufficiently armed force of almost 12,000 Orakzai men was gathering at Kharappa, near Khanki Valley. As a precautionary measure, a preliminary attack was thought of and discussed, but attacking such a large force without administrative and logistical support was not advised at the time. Things remained quiet until two days later when, on 27 August 1897, the Orakzais attacked all the posts along the Samana ridge. The very first attack was made right after daybreak and the Samana Suk, a post almost one and a half kilometre west of Fort Cavagnari, was targeted. The border police, constituting of Pathans, withdrew from the post, choosing to save their own lives. Inside Fort Cavagnari, Major Des Voeux, the second-in-command in the 36th Sikhs, and 150 Indian soldiers stood prepared for an impending attack.

Upon receiving a distress message, Lieutenant Colonel John Haughton, along with two British officers and 130 men, immediately set out for Fort Cavagnari to reinforce it. Lieutenant Colonel Haughton always knew the importance of the forts; therefore, even with a scarcity of men, he always took bold decisions that he thought necessary for the protection of the forts.

When the party led by Lieutenant Colonel Haughton arrived at Fort Cavagnari, he immediately withdrew the troops inside the fort after assessing that they were heavily outnumbered. After they had dealt with Samana Suk, the Orakzais opened fire on Fort Cavagnari from almost a kilometre away. Instantly, Haughton charged two young officers with the task of checking this fire. Three to four hundred yards west of Fort Cavagnari a hillock known as Piquet Hill – this was the point chosen for this action. The officers retreated shortly afterwards, though, since one of them had been shot at and was severely wounded. Shortly afterwards, in the afternoon hours, the Orakzais attacked the eastern part of the Samana range as well. They began to fire at Fort Lockhart from a distance. As a consequence, half of the men Lieutenant Colonel Haughton had taken along with him to Fort Cavagnari had to be sent back to Fort Lockhart as reinforcements.

The Orakzais continued their attempts to capture the forts and withdrew only after last light. The day was saved, but the apprehension of impending attacks kept the 36th Sikhs awake at nights. Though a major attack was not carried out by Orakzais for the next few days, they continued sniping at posts and carrying out minor raids only to inflict casualties.

The next major attack came on 3 September 1897. At first light, a large force of Orakzais began to advance towards Fort Cavagnari from the west. As soon as information about it reached Lieutenant Colonel Haughton, he at once sent reinforcements to strengthen Fort Cavagnari and the Saragarhi post. Heavy firing began from both sides only within a few yards of Fort Cavagnari. The soldiers of the 36th were relying on the thorn abattis[2] placed around the perimeter of the fort walls to slow the enemy down. However, a few Orakzais made a dash towards the abattis and set it on fire. As it burned, the smoke clouds rose up and surrounded the fort, reducing the visibility of the soldiers inside. Sensing the need of the hour, two Sikh soldiers, Sepoy Harnam Singh and Sepoy Sundar Singh, in a display of absolute courage, volunteered to rush outside and put out the fire. Facing heavy enemy fire at close range, these two brave soldiers put out the fire not once but twice under cover fire – this was one of the many gallant acts of 36th Sikhs. The two sepoys were later awarded for their bravery.

This is hardly where the chronicle of such brave acts performed by the Sikh soldiers ceases. It was on the same day that another act of valour was performed. Fearing an

---

2 A thorn abattis was a field fortification made of the branches of trees laid in a row, interlaced or tied with wire, with the sharpened tops directed outwards towards the enemy to act as an obstacle in case the enemy tried to sneak inside the fort.

attack in the dark, a pile of wood outside the fort walls was required to be lit to illuminate the battlefield. Two sepoys, Wariam Singh and Gulab Singh, volunteered to carry out this perilous task. The two young Sikh soldiers leapt over the walls of the fort and ran towards the enemy, lit the fire successfully and returned to the fort without getting killed. For this gallant display of courage, they too were later awarded.

The next morning, the Orakzais withdrew beyond the firing range of weapons. After keeping the troops engaged for a while, they withdrew completely and disappeared, only to return and attack in the night. Following their tactics to the letter, on the next morning the Orakzais withdrew again. Demoralized and disheartened by the lack of any considerable success against the British, however, they turned to the Afridi tribesmen to ask for their support. Both the tribes were aware of the fact that one would need the other in fulfilling a cause that was common to both.

Meanwhile, as the tribesmen were uniting to increase their strength, the British were sending reinforcements of almost 2,500 men, who arrived at Hangu on 7 September. From there, the reinforcement was sent to Fort Lockhart to strengthen its defences. A close reconnaissance was carried out on 9 September from the Samana Suk in which the British officers learnt that a considerably large force of Orakzais and Afridis combined had assembled in the surrounding valley. An attack on this force was not considered a wise option. Neither of the sides engaged in any activity on that day. However, the British discovered from carrying out yet another reconnaissance on 10 September, that more tribesmen had joined the force.

Now that they were a considerably large force, the tribesmen made another clever move. They began their march eastwards towards Hangu through the Khanki Valley on 11 September. When this became known to them, an alarmed British force sent back the reinforcements that had earlier arrived at Fort Lockhart towards Hangu in order to engage the enemy and check their advance. Once these men had left, the shrewd tribesmen once again turned back to attack the Samana forts. The 36th Sikhs still holding the Samana forts were, at Fort Lockhart, only 168 in number, with all ranks answering to Lieutenant Colonel Haughton and another officer; 175 at Fort Cavagnari, with all ranks answering to Major Des Voeux and three other officers; 20 men and a non-combatant housekeeper under Havildar Ishar Singh at Saragarhi; 44 men at the Sangar post; and 20 to 30 men in all other minor forts on the Samana ridge. On the night of 11 September, the tribesmen attacked the Sangar post in skirmishes. The 44 brave soldiers holding the post repelled the attack. On the morning of 12 September, the tribesmen started to gather on the east and west sides of the Saragarhi post, soon surrounding it completely. Their intent was clear – isolation. In the previous attacks on the Samana forts, Saragarhi had proven its worth in timely relaying messages between the two forts, allowing Lieutenant Colonel Haughton to reinforce Fort Cavagnari in time. Therefore, the new objective of the tribesmen lay in between the two major forts. The isolation of Saragarhi began after first light when a large number of Afridis and Orakzais swarmed up the ridge and steadily began to take positions around it even as the 21 Sikh soldiers inside remained unaware of the danger surrounding them. Fort Gulistan was severed from Fort Lockhart as hordes of tribesmen concentrated around Saragarhi. A historic battle, one that would find a worthy place among the pages of history, was only moments away.

10

The Final Call of Duty

'How many infidels?' the leader of the tribesmen asked.

'Twenty one Sikhs and one *Musalman*,' replied an Afridi.

'How many of our brothers have been slain?' the leader asked another man.

'Five hundred, and the count is on,' answered a discouraged voice.

The fallen gate of the fort was still aflame. In the open space in front of the barracks, the tribesmen slowly gathered, edging their way towards the opening. 'Only twenty one...' the leader murmured almost inaudibly, 'burn them... Burn the post.' However, in the dead silence that had fallen inside the fort, nobody dared to carry out his order. All eyes were fixed on the motionless Sikh, Havildar Ishar Singh, who lay in front of them. The Pathans climbed over the walls and the parapets to catch a glimpse of the man whose roaring voice still rang in their ears. His motionless visage reflected tranquillity, an expression of fulfilment and acceptance, even as a drop of blood trickled down from the circumference of his kara. Ishar Singh had done his duty, as had all his brothers who lay there with him.

'Shall I lay their turbans at your feet like you wanted?' One of the Pathans asked his leader, finally breaking the silence.

'No need for that anymore,' murmured the leader, unmoving. He then turned to his awestruck men and shouted, 'What are you waiting for? Burn everything and be done with it,' before stomping out of the post in a hurry.

~

As a response to the ongoing situation in Tirah, the British had planted Sikhs along the border after they had learnt that both were hereditary foes. They had also been impressed by the exemplary bravery the Sikhs had displayed on numerous occasions and did not have to think twice about putting their faith in these turbaned men. After the battle of Saragarhi, the whole world was left in awe of the 21 Sikhs who had pitted themselves against the rifles of 10,000 Pathans in a daring attempt to defend the post to which they had been assigned. However, this was easier said than done. It is now time to relive the moments of the battle as they happened.

The Battle of Saragarhi

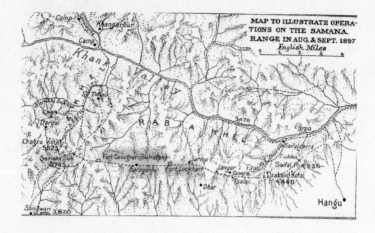

The post of Saragarhi was besieged by Afghan tribesmen on the morning of 12 September 1897, hence cutting off all communication between Fort Lockhart and Fort Cavagnari, and neither Lieutenant Colonel Haughton nor Major De Voeux were able to move out in the open to reinforce the 21 men at Saragarhi as thousands of tribesmen had positioned themselves between Saragarhi and the forts on its either side. The post was now on its own.

With numerical superiority on their side, the Pathans attempted to rush the post in the beginning of the attack, with scores of standards flying, ready to raze everything in their path in the inferno of their discontentment. By then, the soldiers inside the post had already been warned and stood prepared to face this onslaught of more than 10,000 Pathans. Havildar Ishar Singh judged the gravity of the situation at hand and took command without delay. A seasoned soldier, he knew how to encourage the 20 men relying on him for leadership. He is said to have quoted Guru Gobind Singh's verses about how each of them was equivalent to 125,000 foes, and the Pathans they had to fight were not even a fraction of it. He reminded them about the greatness of Maharaja Ranjit Singh, and the fact that it was his legacy they needed to honour that day. He cited the tale of the brave Hari Singh Nalwa, who had fought the Afghans in these very hills not long ago[1]. His words were enough to ignite a fire inside the 20 young Sikh soldiers to give the impending fight their all, thereby creating military history.

Before an all-out attack, the Pathans offered the Sikh soldiers an opportunity to surrender in return for safe passage. However, no offer could lure Havildar Ishar Singh or any of his men. Singh knew that he had to hold the enemy for a few hours until Lieutenant Colonel Haughton could receive reinforcements and they were therefore ready to defend their posts until their deaths. Unsuccessful in their efforts, the aggravated tribesmen

---

1 Hari Singh Nalwa (1791-1837) was Commander-in-Chief of the Sikh Khalsa Army, the army of the Sikh empire during the rule of Maharaja Ranjit Singh. He is known for his role in the conquests of Kasur, Sialkot, Attock, Multan, Kashmir, Peshawar and Jamrud. He is also the founder of Haripur city in Pakistan, which is named after him. Sardar Hari Singh Nalwa is considered to be the only person to have ever completely controlled the Khyber Pass for as long as he did, beginning with the battle at Kasur in 1807 to the taking of Jamrud in 1836. He was well known for his wit and superior knowledge of warfare tactics.

now told the soldiers that they would not survive even for a few minutes if the Pathans charged at them. This, too, did not budge the determined soldiers of Saragarhi. The tribesmen then began to charge at the fort in order to conquer the fort before reinforcements could arrive. Soon, the valley began to echo with the deafening blasts of thousands of Jezails and Henry-Martinis. The Sikhs aimed their rifles at the incoming horde and when the enemy was within effective range of their weapons, they opened fire on Havildar Ishar Singh's order, shouting their war cry of '*Bole so nihaal…sat sri akaal!*'. Wave after wave of Pathans on the frontlines fell and the ones behind them scrambled to find cover. The battle had begun.

The Pathans, who had seemed in a hurry to take down the post just a little while ago, now took cover behind rocks and in defiles where the bullets could not reach them. Using groundcover, the tribesmen began to fire incessantly at the fort even as the battlefield in front of them was sprinkled with dead bodies from the first attack. A firefight ensued, but the Sikhs had to be very careful while using their ammunition as every soldier had only 400 rounds to sustain him in this bloody battle.

In the meantime, Signalman Gurmukh Singh used their heliograph machine to send a message to Lieutenant Colonel John Haughton that they were under attack. While he was distressed to hear this, Haughton replied that it was impossible for him to send reinforcements at the time as they would not be able to break through the intervening hordes of Pathans.

Havildar Ishar Singh then had Gurmukh Singh send a single word as a reply – 'Understood'. This reply spoke volumes about Havildar Ishar Singh's stature and his maturity at the time.

In the midst of the battle, two Pathans sneaked towards the fort walls, moving along defiles under cover fire. Upon reaching one of the walls, they began to make attempts to break it down. As the breach in the wall widened with each passing moment, Havildar Ishar Singh finally noticed it and placed a handful of his soldiers there to welcome the trespassers with their bayonets. Those who trespassed met their death in a fierce hand-to-hand battle until a pile of dead Afghans were choking the opening. Irritated and dispirited, the tribesmen withdrew behind cover. They had received quite a disheartening blow as the battle they thought they would win within minutes had gone on for more than three hours.

Meanwhile, from a distance, an anxious Lieutenant Colonel John Haughton, the commanding officer of 36th Sikhs, saw his 21 men fighting against incredible odds but was also relieved to know that it was Sikhs – under the able Havildar Ishar Singh's command – who held this vulnerable post. At about midday, Havildar Ishar Singh had Gurmukh send a message to Lieutenant Colonel Haughton stating, 'I am down to half my men but the remainder now have two weapons each and so a larger share of ammunition.' This message from Havildar Ishar Singh motivated his commanding officer enough that he decided to send a sortie towards the Saragarhi post.

Hence, Lieutenant Munn, an officer of the 36th, with a small party of soldiers from the Royal Irish Regiment were sent to try to create a diversion by firing at the enemy encircling Saragarhi from long-range rifles like their Lee-Metfords. This was done as ordered, but to no avail. The tribesmen were in the thousands and their focus was solely on Saragarhi.

While the troops in the two main forts were formulating various ways in which to safeguard their signals post, another attempt to breach the wall at Saragarhi had begun. By then, the remaining Sikh soldiers had managed to inflict a great number of casualties on the tribesmen. The incessant firing from the Afghans had not prevented the young soldiers from shooting down their targets. It is a testament to their battle-readiness that even when they were in thousands, the tribesmen didn't attempt another all-out attack against the Sikhs, fearing another setback. However, Saragarhi's defence was wearing thin, and with the Afghans pressing in from all sides, at about three in the afternoon, Havildar Ishar Singh had Signalman Gurmukh Singh notify their commanding officer that their ammunition was running short. It was then that Lieutenant Colonel Haughton and Lieutenant Munn once again attempted to create a diversion or a breakthrough. Such was the plight of this commanding officer that as much as he desired to help his men, he could do nothing but remain a terribly anxious spectator to this unmatched display of valour by his men.

Even as the battle raged, another vulnerable point of the Saragarhi post caught the attention of the tribesmen – the wooden gate studded with iron, which was not big enough to be unsurpassable and, with adequate effort, could be brought down. With utter disregard for their safety, parties of tribesmen charged towards the wooden gate with bundles of brushwood which were lit to set the gate on fire. The first two attempts to bring the gate down were rendered unsuccessful by the brave soldiers. But the Afghans kept coming, making their way through the dead bodies of their brethren. Considerably reduced in numbers, the remaining Sikhs brought calculated fire upon an advancing enemy as best as they could. With each falling Pathan their ammunition depleted but their spirit remained undaunted even as they held their ground alongside their fallen brothers. The air rang with the sound of hundreds of bullets and Havildar Ishar Singh's battle cry as he rained bullets upon the advancing tribesmen. A historical saga was in the making – a spectacular feat of bravery, leadership and military resilience. It was the 'last stand' of 21 gallant Sikh men. Years ago, the Pathans had met a similar defeat on their own soil when General Hari Singh Nalwa of Maharaja Ranjit Singh's army had crushed them in battle. The Sikhs at Saragarhi, thus, carried a rich heritage in their blood and they had done all they could to live up to it.

Hours passed and the battle still continued. With limited ammunition, the remaining Sikhs fired only when the enemy came into the effective range of their rifles. An attempt to bring down the gate was made again, even as the breach in the wall was widening. Those at Fort Cavagnari could see the breach being made but the smoke rising from burning brushwood had rendered their heliograph warning messages ineffective. Critically injured Sikhs who could still manage to lift a rifle took some of their final shots before they succumbed to their injuries. Still composed under the stress of a losing battle, a competent Havildar Ishar Singh ran from man to man, motivating them to give their best as he quoted their Guru's teachings. However, even to Havildar Ishar Singh, it had now become obvious that the end was rapidly approaching.

Meanwhile, in a final attempt to reinforce the party at Saragarhi, Lieutenant Colonel Haughton with Lieutenant Munn and 90 Sikhs had advanced only thousand yards towards the post when they realized that it was too late. The wall had been breached and the half-burnt gate, which was riddled and torn by rifle fire, had also fallen. A large section of the wall weakened by the breach had caved into an underground tunnel, providing the tribesmen with an opportunity to rush inside the post. The reinforcement party saw the enemy swarm inside the post through the breach and the doorway and knew that before they would reach Saragarhi, it would all be over. Complying with Havildar Ishar Singh's final command, a young and undeterred Signalman Gurmukh Singh, who had been performing his duty relentlessly, transmitted one last message via the heliograph: 'We are being overrun but will not surrender. Request permission to close down and join the fight.' After receiving the prompt reply of 'permission granted', Sepoy Gurmukh Singh carefully dismantled the heliograph and, having packed it safely, picked up his weapon and joined the fight. By the time the Pathans swarmed inside the fort, only five of the 21 soldiers remained standing. Displaying leadership of the highest calibre, Havildar Ishar Singh commanded his men to fall back and take refuge in the inner part of the fort whilst he remained behind to fight the advancing enemy. However, in a fierce hand-to-hand combat that ensued under an echoing war cry, the remaining soldiers pounced on the tribesmen and took with them as many as they could before they were, at last, martyred. Gurmukh Singh alone is said to have killed 20 Afghans before he fell. From a distance, Lieutenant Colonel Haughton gazed at Saragarhi with a sense of veneration. The battle was over. The 21 brave soldiers and one non-combatant member of the 36th Sikhs lay inside the fort, martyred. They had performed their duty magnificently, defying terrible odds and setting an unparalleled example of loyalty, selfless service and sacrifice. As the seven-hour-long battle concluded, the other two forts had been given enough time to reinforce and fortify their defences. With almost 600 dead, it was a massive setback for the numerically superior tribesmen. After having paid a terrible price, the humiliated tribesmen set the post on fire and retreated into the valley to regroup.

Top and bottom: Ruins of the Saragarhi fort photographed a few days after the battle

As the day once again came to an end in Tirah, a heroic saga had been written. Such were the feats displayed in this epic battle – brought to light by heliograph messages and on-ground witnesses – that it often becomes difficult separating reality from exaggeration. There exists a monument on Samana Spur near Fort Lockhart and a cairn on the site of Saragarhi post which was built by the British Indian Army to commemorate the gallantry of the defenders of Saragarhi, including a plaque inscribed with the names of the 21 heroes. The inscription on it states that the battle 'is a perpetual record of the heroism shown by these gallant soldiers who died at their posts in defence of the post of Saragarhi on 12th September 1987, fighting against overwhelming numbers, thus proving their loyalty and devotion to the sovereign, the Queen Empress of India and gloriously maintaining the reputation of the Sikhs for unflinching courage in the field of battle'.

A grateful British government awarded each of the 21 soldiers of the battle of Saragarhi the 'Indian Order of Merit (3rd Class)', the highest honour equivalent to the Victoria Cross that could be given to an Indian soldier at the time.

The battle of Saragarhi is one of the eight stories of collective bravery published by the United Nations Educational, Scientific and Cultural Organization (UNESCO). The story of this battle was also included in school textbooks in France as one of the most incredible sagas in world military history. The magnificence of this glorious battle was also acknowledged in many written records, some of which will be mentioned as we move to the next chapter, but as of now, we should commit the glorious battle to memory and not let the heroic saga of its 21 brave soldiers fade away with the passage of time.

11

The Aftermath

The heat of the burning walls of Saragarhi was felt everywhere in British India as well as in England where a telegraph delivered the news of this heroic episode to the queen in an ongoing parliament session which made the queen say, 'The British, as well as the Indians, are proud of the 36th Sikh Regiment. It is no exaggeration to record that the armies which possess the valiant Sikhs cannot face defeat in war.'[1] Major Des Voeux, the officer who was the second-in-command of the 36th Sikhs who had witnessed the entire battle had the following to say: 'Twenty-one men of mine fought like demons. One brave fellow held out in the guard room, and killed twenty of the enemy. He could not be conquered, and at last was burned at his post. These men died the death of heroes, and though the

---

1   Singh, Harinder, (Retd) Vice Admiral, *Sikh Soldier Volume 5*.

annals of the native army of India are full of brave deeds, these men gave up their lives in devotion to their duty.'[2]

Soon, the story of this saga had spread like wildfire and reached every native soldier in every British regiment, serving as a motivating factor for the other troops who were to fight the battles of the Tirah Campaign. When General Sir Arthur Power Palmer, the then Commander-in-Chief of the British Indian Army, learnt about the Battle of Saragarhi, he said, 'The conduct displayed by the twenty one men of the 36th Sikh Regiment was characteristic of the nation's tradition. It should be kept as an example to others, in order to show how brave men should behave when facing fearful odds.'[3]

Words of praises for the 21 Sikhs soon flooded the newspapers and there was not a single British officer who didn't add to it. 'You are never disappointed when you are with the Sikhs. Those twenty one soldiers all fought to the death. That bravery should be within all of us. Those soldiers were lauded in Britain and their pride went throughout the Indian Army. Inside every Sikh should be this pride and courage. The important thing is that you must not get too big-headed, it is important to be humble in victory and to pay respect to the other

2 Bedi, Harchand Singh, 'Saragarhi will live forever in the golden pages of Sikh history', www.panthic.org.
3 *The Times*, 17 April 1902.

side,' wrote Colonel John Douglas Slim[4] in praise of the martyrs of Saragarhi.

We can only try to imagine the plight of a Commanding Officer who had to see his men defend a post with their lives and could do nothing to help them. The nights he spent introspecting shows the qualities that likely earned him the loyalty of his battalion, as his own account of the events show. In letters to his wife dated 13 and 15 September 1897 from Fort Lockhart, Lieutenant Colonel John Haughton expressed his feelings on the matter[5]:

> Yesterday was a terrible day, for I saw twenty-one of our gallant men slaughtered at Saragarhi, and was unable to do anything to prevent it. On the 11th great numbers of the enemy were seen going off in the direction of Hangu; and the General, being fearful for the safety of the small camp there, went off with his force in the evening to save Hangu. His force went down by the Saifuldarra road, or, rather, along the hills that way. They were engaged with the enemy from 10 p.m. to 4.30 the next morning; we could see the fight going on, but could do nothing. I hear we had only about two or three killed, and

---

4 Slim, John Douglas, 'Second Annual "Portraits of Courage" Lecture' hosted by the Maharaja Duleep Singh Centenary Trust, London: The Imperial War Museum.
5 Yate, Major A.C., *The Life of Lieutenant-Colonel John Haughton*, London: John Murray, 1900.

the enemy had fifteen or sixteen. The situation at 9 a.m. on the 12th was as follows – The enemy was in great force on the next hill beyond Sangar (where there used to be a police post called Gogra). Another force, numbering many thousands, appeared on the hills at Saragarhi (that is, between this and Gulistan), and there were a lot more between here and Saragarhi, below the crests of the hills. They simply swarmed on the hills near Saragarhi, which post they surrounded at a short distance, and kept firing at. At twelve o'clock Saragarhi signalled that they had one sepoy killed and one Naik wounded, and three rifles broken by the enemy's bullets. Mr Munn took out twelve men of the Royal Irish (who had been left here sick and as signalers), and tried to fire long-range volleys at the enemy, who were visible from here, though sheltered by rocks from the Saragarhi fort. We saw the enemy make at least two assaults on the post, but they were driven back. At three o'clock I came to the determination, at all costs, to try and make some diversion; so, as soon as possible afterwards, Mr. Munn and I with ninety-eight rifles went out, leaving seventy-three men to defend Fort Lockhart. We had to go very cautiously, as our spies reported a strong force of Afridis below the hills, to the right of the road between this and Saragarhi. We had only gone about three-quarters of a mile when we saw Saragarhi taken by the enemy. Of course it is difficult to say what occurred, but from our own observations and from reports, it seems that the enemy managed to break down the door of the post (a wooden one – a fearful mistake), and then our poor men ran down from the parapet to defend the doorway... I am not sure whether the above is quite correct – that is, whether the door was broken in or not; but Major Des Voeux, who was surrounded at Gulistan, saw the Pathans at Saragarhi making a hole in a dead angle in the wall. They got in there, and our men ran down to defend the hole, and the enemy immediately swarmed over the walls. The end was not long, though it is said that one poor fellow defended himself in the guard-room and shot twenty of the enemy inside the post. The brutes then set the place on fire.

No sooner had the Saragarhi post fallen did the enemy divert their attention to Fort Cavagnari, which was cut off from Fort Lockhart, making it much more vulnerable given the recent developments. There was much at stake for the Afghans who had lost alarming numbers in an unexpectedly fierce battle. While the battle of Saragarhi was still being fought, another group of Pathans had occupied Samana Suk and Piquet Hill by forenoon and were disturbingly close to Fort Gulistan, where Major De Voeux and his men stood prepared to face them. The attack on Fort Gulistan commenced at about four in the afternoon on 12 September, after Saragarhi fell. Major De Voeux positioned his men along the defences and on each bastion, with a sentry to keep a special watch on any attempt by the Pathans to breach the outer wall, a lesson they had learnt after witnessing the same happening at Saragarhi. Incessant firing that began and continued through the night of 12 September until dawn the next day brought no respite; in fact, it was observed in the morning that the tribesmen had managed to take defensive positions close to the fort walls along its entire periphery.

To effectively make use of initiative, i.e. making the first move keeping in mind the enemy's strategies, Major De Voeux decided that a raid needed to be carried out against the Pathans. As a result, Havildar Kala Singh, a motivated non-commissioned officer (NCO) who volunteered for the raid, went out with a handful of his men at about eight in the morning and crept to the south-west corner where they, with their bayonets, charged at the enemy hiding in the folds of the ground. The Pathans, however, were quick on the uptake and began to fire at them, forcing them to take cover. At this juncture, another NCO named Havildar Sunder Singh along with eleven other men hurdled over the walls to provide them with support, and both parties together charged at the Pathans and drove them away before successfully returning to the fort. Men who were gravely injured in this raid were also brought back inside the hornwork – a testament to the commendable quality of the Sikhs to leave no man behind. Later, two of these raiding soldiers succumbed to their injuries.

The valiant acts of the day had only begun, further motivated by the previous day's legendary events. The men at Fort Gulistan bravely stood their guard and fearlessly defended the fort walls; even the wounded never left their posts. Of course, the raid had produced beneficial results. Where the tribesmen had yet not recovered from the previous day's losses, this raid by the Sikh soldiers cowed them before they could attempt an all-out assault. The incessant fire, however, continued from their side. In the meantime, General Yeatman Biggs had received intelligence that Fort Gulistan was under attack. He at once flagged off a signalling party towards Doaba to inform Major De Voeux that they would have to hold the fort until 14 September after which reinforcements would arrive. On the 13th, field guns began their bombardment in the Miranzai Valley from the direction of Doaba. This sudden fire support added to the morale of the defenders, but their circumstances did not change throughout the night. Even as fatigue, hunger and thirst crept in, nobody budged or lost heart. On this very night, General Yeatman Biggs, with almost 1,800 infantrymen and four artillery guns, left from Hangu and reached Samana Hills on the morning of 14 September.

In the meantime, the Afridis and Orakzais had begun to make an attempt to lay siege on Fort Gulistan just as they had done at Fort Saragarhi. Ten to twelve thousand of the tribesmen had gathered on top of Saragarhi and Piquet Hill to surround the fort. However, the fire of field guns that began around nine in the morning had forced the tribesmen to retreat to the Khanki valley. When the reinforcements under General Biggs arrived, they first secured Fort Lockhart, following which a party from the fort sallied forth and opened fire on the retreating enemy. Lieutenant Colonel John Haughton and his men joined the relief force and began to advance towards Fort Gulistan, unaware at this juncture whether or not Gulistan was still safe and held by their own troops. It was only after the Pathans were driven off from the top of Saragarhi that the relieving party observed that Fort Gulistan was still safe.

The relieving party under Lieutenant Colonel Haughton then charged at the thousands of Pathans who still swarmed around Fort Gulistan. On seeing the reinforcements closing in from the direction of Fort Lockhart, the Pathans drew-off towards Samana Suk in the west. As they retreated, Major De Voeux saw an opportunity and the Pathans soon came under the effective range of the defenders' weapons. In fact, this volley of bullets from the fort killed many Pathans before they retreated to the valley. The attack on the Samana forts had failed and Orakzais and Afridis combined had lost about 400 men with another 600 wounded. Of course, no battle is won without casualties. The 36th Sikhs had also suffered heavy losses, with the 21 Sikhs at Saragarhi and two men, including Havildar Kala Singh who had led the raid on the morning of the 13th, giving up their lives to defend their posts. An officer and 39 men suffered injuries. It is to be noted that Major Des

Voeux's family, who was in the fort during the attack, remained safe and left the fort unhurt.

Fort Gulistan was gallantly defended by the 36th Sikhs for 52 hours before reinforcements arrived. It was a battle that tested the might of Sikh soldiers who were motivated enough to avenge the death of their 21 brothers who had set high standards for others to follow. With images of the Battle of Saragarhi still fresh in their minds, the Sikh soldiers at Fort Gulistan provided tough resistance and made each bullet count. Major Des Voeux, who had two things to worry about – his family and the fort – showed the highest level of leadership qualities in this battle as he cheerfully and steadfastly faced all his troubles and led his men until help arrived.

Of these turbulent hours, Lieutenant Colonel John Haughton wrote[6]:

[A]fter the fall of Saragarhi, its captors went off to help the Pathans at Gulistan, leaving some thousands at Saragarhi, to prevent succour going to Gulistan. They attacked all that day and night. The next morning things were very critical, and Major Des Voeux gave leave to a Havildar and sixteen men, who had volunteered, to make a sortie. These gallant fellows went out of the hornwork gate, ran

---

6 Yate, Major A.C., *The Life of Lieutenant-Colonel John Haughton*, London: John Murray, 1900.

along outside the hornwork and attacked a party of
the enemy who had planted their standards under a
crest of the hill, only about twenty yards beyond the
end of the hornwork. They were having a bad time
of it, when another Havildar and eleven men got
over the end of the hornwork and went to their aid.
This turned the scale, and the gallant little party
drove the enemy back at this point and took three
of their standards. Out of the seventeen who first
went out, eleven were wounded, as well as several
of the second party. When they got back they found
that a wounded man was left behind, and they again
went out and brought him in. Nothing could have
been more gallant. I regret to say that of the two
Havildars one is already dead, and the other, I fear,
cannot live. That sortie had a wonderfully depressing
effect on the enemy, and a splendid effect on all
our men. No assistance could come to Gulistan for
another twenty-four hours, and of course it was a
fearfully anxious time for us at Fort Lockhart. It is
impossible to describe what an anxious time it must
have been for Major Des Voeux… The General sent
a field-battery on the evening of the 13th to the
foot of the hill. Of course it could not get up, but
it sent some shells pretty near the enemy, which,
though they may not have done much harm, had a
good moral effect. During all that night I listened
anxiously, and was very thankful whenever I heard
a shot from Gulistan. We, that night and the night

before, had a few shots fired into us, but it was only what is commonly called 'sniping'. However, at about seven o'clock Mr Munn, with thirty of our men and about a dozen of the Royal Irish, went out and got down to a bit of a hill below Sangar, where we were able to get some good though long-range volleys into the enemy as they retired before the General… I cannot say what damage our volleys did to them, as they were so scattered about over the hillside, but we could see our bullets going all in among them and knocking up the dust… As soon as the enemy had fled from their position beyond Sangar, the General said he must push on hard to Gulistan. So we with our few men raced back to Fort Lockhart, got all the men we had left there out, and, without asking permission, stuck ourselves at the head of the General's force. The enemy were pretty strong at Sangar, and we thought they would fight; so, unfortunately as it turned out, the General determined to shell the place before the infantry advanced. Consequently the enemy disappeared behind the ridge. We thought they would wait there till the advance of our own infantry prevented the guns firing, and would then jump up and give us a busy time. However, when the 36th and 2nd Panjab Infantry advanced over the hill there was not a man left. Poor Saragarhi was absolutely a heap of stones, but amongst the ruins we could distinguish the remains of our poor fellows, hacked to pieces by these fiends. Then, when we got beyond the Saragarhi heights and could see Gulistan, we saw the enemy as thick as peas round it; but they bolted like French partridges as soon as we showed our noses a mile and a half off, and, unfortunately, it was a long time before the guns could get up. When they did get up there were very few of the enemy left within range; and though the guns opened a pretty accurate fire, I don't fancy the enemy could have suffered much. We found our people at Gulistan very cheery. The General is awfully pleased with all our men; I think they have just done splendidly.

As is evident from the conduct of the men who fought from Fort Gulistan on 13 and 14 September, the last stand of the 21 soldiers of Saragarhi had an electrifying effect on the self-esteem of the remaining soldiers of the 36th Sikhs, filling them with a desire for revenge that must have stimulated these brave men to stand their ground against overwhelming odds for so long. The defence of the Samana forts was, therefore, more or less a tribute by the regiment to their fallen brethren.

Honours and memorials

What bigger honour can there be for martyrdom than remembrance? Such was the case with the Battle of Saragarhi, after which the country came together to honour the martyrs. The British Indian government were quick to confer the heroes of the battles with deserved honours, as described in the following extract of an article published in the *London Gazette* in 1898[7]:

> The Governor-General in Council desires especially to express his admiration of the brilliant defence of Fort Gulistan by the 36th Sikhs, and of the post of Saragarhi by a party of twenty men of the same regiment under the command of Havildar Ishar Singh, who died fighting to the last, displaying a heroic devotion which has never been surpassed in the annals of the Indian Army.
>
> [...] His Excellency is of [the] opinion that the operations in question were well planned and skillfully carried out. The march to the relief of Gulistan was performed under very trying circumstances, owing to the heat and to a great scarcity of water en route, but the force successfully accomplished its object with the same gallantry and cheerfulness as have been evinced on every occasion by our troops during the various operations which have recently taken place on the North-West Frontier.
>
> The Commander-in-Chief wishes to draw attention to the admirable conduct and steadiness of the 36th Sikhs, under the command of Lieutenant-Colonel Haughton, during the attack on the various

---

7 *London Gazette*, Issue 26937, pp. 863–864, Fort William: 11 February 1898.

posts held by that regiment on the Samana Range. At Sangar, the small garrison made a sortie and gallantly captured a standard from the enemy, while the brilliant defence of Fort Gulistan by the detachment, under the command of Major Des Voeux, reflects the greatest credit on that officer and the garrison of the post. The Government of India will, His Excellency is assured, appreciate fully the intrepid manner in which the late Havildar Kala Sing[h] led the sortie from the Gulistan Fort, and also the conduct of Havildar Sundar Singh, who assisted his comrades at a critical moment.

The Commander-in-Chief deeply regrets the loss of the garrison of Saragarhi, a post held by 21 men of the 36th Sikhs, and he wishes to record his admiration of the heroism shown by those gallant soldiers. Fighting against over-whelming numbers they died at their post, thus proving their loyalty and devotion to their Sovereign while upholding to the last the traditional bravery of the Sikh nation.

[...] I fully endorse the Major-General's commendation on the defence of Fort Gulistan and the behaviour of all ranks. Major Des Voeux proved himself a gallant and skilful leader, and the Major-General's remarks on this officer's conduct appear to be fully deserved.

I have much pleasure in recommending for the Order of Merit all the non-commissioned officers and men the Major-General has brought to notice.

Meanwhile, in India, in an article published by *The Pioneer* on 2 December 1897, it was stated that the office of the newspaper had raised Rs 10,000 in lieu of donations for a Saragarhi memorial. The article reads:

Dear Sir,

As the subscriptions received by *The Pioneer* on behalf of the proposed memorial to the Sikhs who fell at Saragheri now amount to close on ten thousand rupees, I think it opportune to acquaint the members of the committee of the Fund with the wishes of the subscribers so far as there can be ascertained from letters received by me.

The Fund was originally opened by *The Pioneer* in response to a suggestion that some memorial should be raised to the 21 Sikhs who fell at Saragheri, nothing being said as to the shape which the memorial might properly take. In the interval, however, several suggestions have been made, and these may here be conveniently classified as follows:-

(1) A memorial to be erected at Amritsar and also one at Saragheri.

(2) A memorial to be erected at Amritsar only.

(3) Half the money to be collected to go to a memorial at Amritsar and half to be distributed among the widow and children of those who fell at Saragheri.

(4) The amount to be distributed not to be given in a lump sum, but paid in the form of annuities.

(5)   The Sikhs who took part in the sortie from Fort Gulistan also to be included among beneficiaries of the Fund.

(6)   A grant of land to be secured somewhere in the Punjab, preferably in the new Chenab settlement.

As to the memorial at Amritsar the question may be regarded as settled, in as much as the Government of India have now consented to defray the expense. As to the proposal for a separate monument at Saragheri, I may direct the attention of the Committee to the opinion expressed by General Westmacott, Commanding the 4th Brigade, T.E.F, 'that any memorial erected on the Samana range would certainly be desecrated at some future time.' If the Committee concur in this opinion, then the whole fund becomes available for distribution, and the only question to be decided is as to the number of beneficiaries to be included and the method of distribution. As to the former point, Colonel Haughton himself, Commanding the 36th Sikhs, suggested the inclusion of the men who fell in the sortie from Fort Gulistan, and this opinion will probably commend itself to the other members of the Committee. As to the method of distribution, one correspondent has pointed out that if the money were distributed in a lump sum it might not improbably be dissipated, and he proposes annuities to the immediate heirs. The advantage of an annuity is obvious, but as the purchase price would depend on the ages of the recipients, it would be necessary to have details on this point before the total cost could be estimated. If we suppose 30 heirs, a monthly pension of 3 rupees each would involve an outlay of 1080 rupees per annum. An insurance company might take the risk of such a payment for a lump sum of 13,000 or 14,000 rupees; the precise sum depending on the average age of the recipients. The Fund at present amounts to 10,000 rupees but subscriptions continue to come in and it is not improbable that a total of 12,000 rupees or 13,000 rupees will be attained.

There is finally the suggestion that the Punjab Government should be asked to give a grant of land where the beneficiaries of the Fund might be settled. If the Committee favour this suggestion, it would be desirable to open communications with the Punjab Government as early as possible.

Finally, I desire to invite the opinion of the Committee as to whether a date should be fixed when the Fund will be closed, or whether for the time being this should be left indefinite. The Committee may also think it advisable to appoint a regular Secretary to the Fund.

I am, Yours faithfully,
Maitland H. Park,
Officiating Editor, *The Pioneer*

To commemorate the bravery of the 21 martyrs of the Battle of Saragarhi, three memorials were erected – one at Saragarhi, the venue of the battle; the second at Firozepur; and the third at Amritsar. The memorial at Amritsar, situated opposite the Government Higher Secondary School, Town Hall, was unveiled on 14 February 1902.

The memorial gurudwara in Amritsar

The memorial gurdwara at Ferozepur was built at a cost of Rs 27,118 by the British to honour these brave soldiers. It was inaugurated in 1904 by Sir Charles Rivaz, the then Lieutenant Governor of Punjab. According to an old article published on 18 January 1904, this inauguration was no ordinary event:

> [It took place] in [the] presence of an imposing assemblage of spectators, numbering fully 5000... with full ceremonial honours. To the dozens of cameras large and small, brought by professional and amateur photographs, a scene of real picturesqueness presented itself. In the centre, dominating all else by the size and brilliance, stood Saragarhi monument – a glistering snow-white Sikh temple in that elaborately ornate style of architecture which eastern custom has appropriated to memorials of the dead. Photography, insensible to the charms of colour, responsive only to beauty of the form, had here and ideal subject. From the base to the topmost pinnacle, a height of 60 or 70 feet, the marble like purity of surface shone with but a single tone in the golden rays of the afternoon sun. It seems but fitting that the Sikh temple should be designed by a Sikh artist, Bhai Ram Singh, the gifted Vice Principal of the Mayo School of Art, Lahore, has unconsciously handed down to posterity his own name as well as the names of the Saragarhi heroes, by creating a piece of poetic architecture that will henceforth rank as one of the lights of the Punjab. When the future visitor to Ferozepur stands in wondering admiration before this gleaming edifice,

with its eight milk-white walls in the true octagonal symmetry, surmounted by a flated dome pinnacled in gold; when he marks the gracefulness of the four staircases leading up on four sides, north, south, east and west, to for entrance porches, each canopied by a flated, gold pinnacled dome in sympathy with the main design; when beneath the shade of the four porches, he notes the carved splendour of the four Shisham doors, each garnished by thirty-two floriated panels; and when having passed through the doors he steps up on richly tessellated Italian marble floor, into an octagonal house of worship, and beholds the lofty dome heavily honeycombed with pendeative ornament – he will surely feel that he is surveying the work of a master artist. And whatever his race and tongue he will know that the memorial is the outcome of a spontaneous glow of admiration, which first found expression in the columns of the *Pioneer* newspaper; for this essential fact is proclaimed to the world in sculptured letters from the four walls of the temple in four different languages – in English, in Urdu, in Gurmukhi and in Hindi. Thus:

This monument is erected to the memory of the men of the 36th (Sikh) Regiment of the Punjab Infantry who fell in the heroic defence of Fort Saragarhi on the 12th September 1897, and in the gallant sortie from Fort Gulistan on the 13th September 1897:

A spontaneous testimony – the result of voluntary subscriptions collected through the Pioneer newspaper, Allahabad – from the Anglo-Indian and Indian public to the undying glory which these ever memorable feats of arms brought to the soldiers of the Khalsa and the arms of the British Empire.

[...] It remains to mention that the design of the memorial was finally approved after consultation with the Sikh authorities of the Golden Temple at Amritsar, and with then [*sic*] Commander-in-Chief the late Sir William Lockhart; that his Honour the Lieutenant-Governor kindly allowed the memorial to be constructed by the public works department as 'contribution work', the cost of establishment, tools and plant being remitted; and the work of construction was superintended by Bakshi Ram Singh, Executive Engineer, directed by Mr Cockburn, Assistant Engineer, and managed by Ram Lal and Devi Sahi; and that the total sum collected by the *Pioneer* exceeded Rs 30,000, of which Rs 26,000 was expended on the memorial building, and the balance distributed among the widows and orphans of Saragarhi heroes...

To this day, on 12 September every year, this memorial hosts a religious congregation in the morning followed by a reunion of ex-servicemen in the evening.

The memorial gurudwara in Firozpur

Along with the gurdwaras in Amritsar and Firozpur, a cairn was built at the site of Saragarhi.

S.E. of Saragarhi 1930

An old photograph of the cairn built by the British Indian government
at the site of the Battle of Saragarhi

~

Even in the entire gamut of operations being carried
out under the Tirah Campaign, when newspapers
and editorials were flooded with dispatches from their
battlefield correspondents, the noteworthy pens could
not keep from writing the mentions about the epic Battle
of Saragarhi that had awed the British Empire in India.

12

The Tirah Expedition

'When you're wounded and left on Afghanistan's plains,
And the women come out to cut up what remains,
Jest roll to your rifle and blow out your brains
An' go to your Gawd like a soldier.'

– The Young British Soldier, *Rudyard Kipling*

In the nineteenth century, the North West Frontier Province was notoriously unstable, particularly in the year 1897. The attack on the Samana Forts and the fall of the Saragarhi post served as the last straw for the British Indian government, who had long been dealing with skirmishes with the tribes that lived in the unforgiving mountains surrounding Tirah. Before long, the tables in Generals' offices were covered with maps and blow-ups; rifles were cleaned and distributed with on-weapon ammunition; and the lamps burnt longer than usual in the chambers of unit and sub-unit commanders as exhaustive planning for the Tirah Campaign began. The campaign was aimed to exact reparation from the Afridis and the Orakzais for their unprovoked aggression on the Peshawar-Kohat border, and for their attacks on British frontier posts. The British deployed fighting columns to the North West Frontier as a part of the campaign and when they had won their pitched battles, they forced Afghan guerrilla fighters to enter into open warfare by destroying houses and crops. After the tribes had been punished enough, they were forced to enter an agreement of peace. However, the Tirah campaign, considered as the biggest deployment after the revolt of 1857, proved to be one of the most difficult battles fought by the British Indian Army.

The G.O.C.C. dated 8 October 1897 depicts the intent with which the government wished to launch an expedition in the Tirah Valley[1]:

> The Government of India have lived at peace with the Afridi tribe and made an agreement with them, under which the British forts in the Khyber were entrusted to their care. Allowances were paid to the tribe, and arms were issued so that they might be strong in their alliance and friendship with the Government of India, and have the means of forcing turbulent persons to keep the peace. Without any

---

1 Hutchinson, H.D., *The Campaign in Tirah 1897-1898*, London: Macmillan & Co, 1898.

provocation the Afridis, in conjunction with other tribes, have broken their alliance with the British Government, and have attacked and destroyed the forts which their tribe had engaged to guard. Further, they have waged war against our garrisons on the Samana and elsewhere, killing some of the soldiers in the British service, and causing great loss of property. The British Government, confident in its power, cannot sit down quietly under such defiance and outrages, and has been forced by the wanton acts of the Afridis themselves to inflict punishment on them in their own country, and to send a force into Tirah to exact reparation for what has lately taken place. The Afridi soldiers in the service of the Government have given proofs of their loyalty, devotion, and courage on many a hard-fought field, and the value of their services has been fully appreciated by the Government of India. After the most careful consideration of the circumstances connected with the Tirah expedition, the Government of India have decided to show consideration to those Afridi soldiers who wish to keep their engagements, and to excuse them from service in the campaign which the Government have been forced to wage against their fellow-tribesmen. On these grounds alone it has been determined that Afridi soldiers who are serving in the regiments detailed for service on the Peshawar – Kohat border, are not to be employed near the Tirah frontier at the present time, but their services will be utilised elsewhere. The necessary orders to this effect will at once issue. As far as possible care will be taken that the property of those who have not taken part in the raids on British territory is neither confiscated nor destroyed during the time that our troops are engaged in the Orakzai or Afridi territory. This order is to be read and carefully explained to all Afridi soldiers belonging to regiments detailed for service on the Peshawar-Kohat border.

Hence, battle lines had been drawn, signalling the start of a series of hard-fought battles.

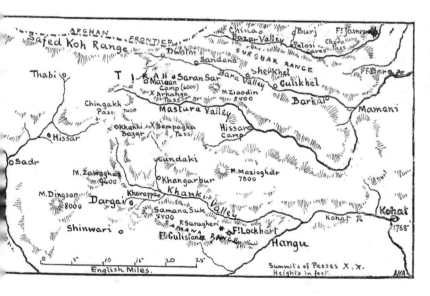

A map of the Tirah Campaign

The Battle of Dargai

By October 1897, after enduring several unprovoked attacks by Afghan tribesmen, the British finally decided to retaliate. The tribesmen had been able to forecast the intended route of the British transport columns since a road up to Chagru Kotal was constantly being improved upon by the British. As a consequence, they had occupied the village of Dargai and the Narik spur along the western boundary of the Chagru Valley, and skilfully dominated the road to Chagru. It became obvious to the British that they would have to launch an attack against the tribesmen to dislodge them from this vantage point as a preliminary measure. The attack began on 18 October as batteries[2] sprang into action against the ridge at Dargai, where the enemy was clustered. This artillery fire, however, had little effect on the tribesmen who took advantage of the excellent cover provided by the rocks. The British troops[3] then hustled up the steep ascent to reach the tribesmen with the 1st Battalion of the 3rd Gurkha Rifles leading, and the King's Own Scottish Borderers and the Northamptons coming up behind them.

---

2 A sub-unit of artillery is a battery. A battery has six artillery guns.
3 *see* Appendix.

The 1st Battalion of the 3rd Gurkhas

Finally, at midday, the troops made a final rush across the open country and charged at the tribesmen. The brave Gurkhas were gallantly led by Major Rose, Captain Bateman-Champain, and Lieutenant Beynon, as they dashed up the steep slopes as fast as their legs could carry them across the steep slopes. With the Scottish Borderers following close behind, and soon, the enemy withdrew and retreated down the slopes. Thirteen Gurkha soldiers and six men of the Scottish Borderers were wounded in this operation and, surprisingly, only two died.

The Mountain Battery in action in Tirah

After the success of this operation, the commander felt it prudent to withdraw these forces as they were isolated and it was difficult for the rear columns to supply them with administrative support, with water rations being a critical issue in particular. General Lockhart felt that the presence of the British forces at Dargai would reveal their intended transport route. As a result, the troops vacated the Dargai heights. On 20 October, when the British columns began to move, the tribesmen decided to attempt a reoccupation of the heights and that, too, with considerable numbers. Amidst the excellent gunning by batteries, the Gordons, two companies of the Borderers and the 15th Sikhs covered the withdrawal of the British troops from Chagru Kotal, but the tribesmen were determined and pressed their attack in spite of severe loss inflicted on them. The fight went on till late in the night and after the tribesmen suffered heavy losses, they finally let the forces retreat without any more incidents. Five Victoria Crosses were awarded for the action, but it also resulted in the death of 4 officers and 34 enlisted men, with 14 officers and 147 enlisted men wounded. The defences at Dargai were destroyed before the troops retired, and the village was burned. The enemy finally accepted defeat and evacuated the Dargai Heights. Among the British Indian troops, the dead were buried with honours at Shinauri and the wounded received treatment at the base hospitals.

The Attack on Sampagha Pass

Now that the Dargai Heights were safely under British control, the Tirah Expeditionary Force could advance with comparatively less resistance. The 2nd Division, that is, the Northamptons, the 36th Sikhs and the No. 9 Mountain Battery, began their advance towards the Khanki valley on the 21 October. The forces camped at an extensive plateau on the north bank of the Khanki River, opposite the village of Khangarbur. Here, necessary space was available to set up large camps and its distance from the nearest tribal lands offered its own security against the prowling raids of Pathans. Since Khangarbur village was inhabited by Afridis, they opened fire on the British columns but the same was checked well by the Mountain Battery. The real difficulty for the forces, however, lay in the march from Shinauri to this campsite which was almost 20 kilometres away. As time went by, the 1st and 2nd Divisions finally assembled in Khanki valley after immense difficulty. They had planned an attack on the Sampagha Pass that was supposed to commence on 29 October, but the Orakzais and Afridis had assembled a force of no less than 12,000 men on the Sampagha Pass and held it in their grip. The storming of Sampagha Pass was not going to be easy for the British.

The whistling of bullets flying over the camp from the guns of the hidden tribesmen kept the British awake and anxious throughout the night of 25 October. The numbers of casualties were adding up. An officer was dreadfully hit by a Snider bullet that shattered the bones in his left arm and had to be amputated. Others barely escaped injury as bullets shot by them or simply made holes in their tents. Peace fell over the valley only when the 3rd Gurkhas and Nabha Infantry, in a voluntary mission, went to occupy the hills from where the fire was being directed at British in the night.

A camp of the 36th Sikhs

The much-awaited advance on Sampagha Pass began on 28 October. The 36th Sikhs and the Northampton Regiment commenced their march as the advance party at 5 a.m., followed by the Yorks, half-battalion 4th Gurkhas and half-battalion 3rd Sikhs, and by 9 a.m. the force was in full march up the valley with the First Division on the left of the line and the Second Division on the right. The main body of the First Division was headed by Sir William Lockhart himself. The tribesmen offered negligible resistance barring a few small attacks on the flanks and the British force halted on a ground close to the Sampagha Pass to pass the night and devise a final plan of attack for the next day. The 2nd Brigade was entrusted with the responsibility of leading the main attack at 5 a.m., with the 4th Brigade meant to support the 2nd on its right flank, and the 3rd Brigade to follow the 2nd as a reserve. The protection of the batteries was the responsibility of the 1st Brigade. By 7 a.m., the attack had been launched, with all forces in their various positions. In this battle – that ended in a win for the British – the Queen's lost one man, the Gurkhas two, the 36th Sikhs two and no. 5 Mountain Battery lost their Commanding Officer and few others were wounded. The tribesmen were entirely expelled from the pass by 11.15 a.m. when the firing completely ceased. Now that the Sampagha Pass had been captured by the British, the Mastura valley lay ahead with the Arghana Pass – which lay in Tirah proper and was inhabited by tribesmen – only eight kilometres away.

The Attack on the Arghana Pass

After the capture of the Sampagha Pass, the British set their sights on taking back the Arghana Pass from the Afghans. However, this was easier said than done, as it would be the first time the British would be scaling such heights. Hence, the entire day after the battle at Sampagha was spent pushing up supplies for troops and to reconnoitre the approaches to Arghana. Such was the difficulty offered by the terrain that Sir Lockhart himself said, 'My great difficulty was the want of food, some corps having absolutely nothing in hand, and the steep and narrow track over the pass delaying the arrival of supplies. But by redistributing what there was, and making use of what could be collected from neighbouring villages, each man was eventually provided with two days' rations.'[4] Nevertheless, the Sappers, Miners and Pioneers toiled continuously to improve the road.

In the attack on Arghana, the 2nd Division got the opportunity to lead under the command of General Yeatman Biggs. The 4th Brigade, supported by the 3rd Gurkha Scouts and a company of Sappers, formed the advance guard, which was followed by the 3rd Brigade. Further in line were the 1st Division and 2nd Brigade with the task of turning the left flank of tribesmen. The attack commenced in the morning of 31 October with the infantry occupying one objective after another under the cover fire of 36 guns that kept raining bullets on the tribesmen. Soon, the Afghans were seen retreating and, by 11 a.m., the Arghana Pass was entirely captured by the British. In this attack, Captain Searle of the 36th Sikhs suffered a gunshot wound along with five other soldiers. Two days after this battle, the tribesmen retaliated and the troops suffered a few casualties. Later, peace was partially restored after which the tribesmen returned to guerrilla warfare, carrying out small and random attacks after every few days. An attack on the Sikh and Gurkha battalions on 9 November, an ambush on the Dorsets and the Sikhs, sneak attacks in the winter after fog and mist descended on the valley after 11 December onwards, kept the British busy but, finally, as the weather improved, even the Khyber Pass was captured. Sir Lockhart could now negotiate with the

---

4 Hutchinson, H.D., *The Campaign in Tirah 1897-1898*, London: Macmillan & Co, 1898.

tribesmen from a position of strength; these negotiations went on till June of 1898 and ended in a pact where the tribesmen agreed to hand over 8,000 breech-loading rifles and pay an indemnity of Rs 50,000 in return of monthly allowances being paid to the tribal chiefs by the British.

A camp of the 36th Sikhs in Maidan, ahead of the Arghana Pass

This was the Campaign of Tirah in brief. It was a war that offered countless opportunities to many brave men, both native and English, to prove their mettle in the battlefield, though it wasn't without significant losses of man and beast. Fighting in the North West Frontier Province was full of difficulties and the victory was not an easy one but, for the time being, the tribesmen had been vanquished. The British government knew that there would once again be unrest in future, but fighting in Tirah had taught them enough about guerrilla tactics and mountain warfare that they began to prepare to thwart such a possibility.

Afterword

THE LEGACY OF THE 36TH SIKHS

In a letter to the authors, Lt Gen S.K. Jha, PVSM, AVSM, YSM, SM, Colonel of the Sikh Regiment was all praises for his illustrious battalion:

With my chest swollen with pride, as Colonel of the most decorated Regiment of the Indian Army, I take the opportunity to pay our homage to gallant martyrs of the Regiment. History is replete with examples of unmatched gallantry of the Sikhs – descendants of the Guru – born and bred in the din and clatter of battles and living by the highest standards of moral code and ethics. They have always defended the honour of this nation and their valour knows no bounds making them the most feared adversary on the battlefield. I and the entire Regiment shall remain indebted for their selfless service and devotion to duty which has propelled the Regiment and Country to the pinnacles of glory.

The unprecedented and iconic Battle of Saragarhi is a testimony to the indomitable spirit of the Sikh soldier, an epitome of bravery and an unparalleled example of duty and sacrifice. The glorious achievement of handful of our warriors who faced thousands with undaunted courage, defying terrible odds and certain death is in keeping with the motto of our Regiment:

Deh shiva bar mohey ehai
Shubh karman te kabhun na taron,
Nah darun arison jab jaye laroon
Nische kar apni jeet karoon.

[O God give me this boon that I never refrain from doing the righteous act. Therefore, I shall have no fear of the enemy when I go into battle and with determination I will be victorious.]

To commemorate the exemplary courage of these 21 mighty soldiers of the 36th Sikhs in the epic Battle of Saragarhi, our young man in uniform, Nirvan Singh, along with his co-author Professor Kirandeep Singh, has worked tirelessly to collect factual data and chronicled the events concerning the battle with outstanding support provided by 4 Sikh. They have brought out a book that glorifies the spirit of soldiering and sacrifice to the cause. The unique poetic style of writing, along with brief fictional episodes helps build connection with this non-fiction which is commendable.

I compliment them for this noble endeavour and wish them all the very best.

'Waheguru ji ka khalsa, Waheguru ji ki fateh!'

S.K. Jha
Lieutenant General
Colonel of the Sikh Regiment

Colonel S.K. (full name withheld for security reasons), the Commanding Officer of the 4th Battalion of the Sikh Regiment had the following to say about his unit's history:

The Battle of Saragarhi is one of the most important and unusual battles in the history of India and the world in which 21 gallant soldiers of the 36th Sikhs (now 4 Sikh) heroically stood against the massive onslaught of 10,000 Afghan tribesmen defending the post of Saragarhi till their last breath on the historic day of 12 September 1897. The battle and the 21 Khalsa soldiers who fought the battle are forever etched in the minds of all officers and men of the Indian Army and continue to be a guiding light for generations, teaching them the very underlying principle of upholding the ethos of the Regiment by defying odds no matter how terribly stacked against them and emerging victorious even at the peril of their lives.

As Commanding Officer of the unit I hold in the highest regard the unsurpassed devotion and dedication of the martyrs of the unit who from time to time have taught us the sole purpose of each man in uniform and at this juncture, I express gratitude to all soldiers and veterans and the brave Sikh troops who have always overwhelmed me with their unmatched loyalty and fondness towards the unit. I shall forever feel privileged for the responsibility bestowed upon me as a Commanding Officer of the battalion with such glorious history of achievements.

Below is a letter from a young officer currently serving in 4th Battalion, The Sikh Regiment:

With 'passing out' coming closer in the academy, every cadet's uneasiness starts swirling up. Which arm would I get into? Would I get the regiment of my choice? How would the officers in my unit be? These are only some of the questions that pop up while passing out edges closer, and I was no exception to this rule. When the day of declassification came and I was told that 4 Sikh would be my unit, I was elated to know that I had got the regiment I chose. The first thing I was told that night was to read about the Battle of Saragarhi. The more I read about how the 21 Sikhs of the 36th had fought 10,000 Afghans, the more proud I felt at having been selected to serve in 4 Sikh. They showcased both mental courage and the warrior code of the Khalsa by choosing to fight until their deaths, and displayed the highest standards of physical courage by successfully defending waves of enemy combatants for several hours. Their feat quickly spread like a firestorm and they were all awarded the Indian Order of Merit, which was the highest medal given for military exploits to Indian soldiers at the time.

The Battle of Saragarhi was not the only battle in which the 36th Sikhs proved their mettle; they have done so whenever and wherever they were given the chance. The battalion has earned 22 Battle Honours and 4 Theatre Honours till date. In WW-I, the battalion was first sent to China, becoming the first Sikh battalion to be deployed in our neighbouring country. There, the battalion fought in the Siege of Tsing Tao against Germany along with the Japanese Imperial Army. From there, the unit moved to Mesopotamia, where it fought one of the bloodiest battles against the Turks in Mesopotamia and Hai. In the Battle of Hai, 83 per cent of the battalion was martyred, and the battalion was awarded battle honours for both the battles.

In between WW I and WW II, the battalion moved to different stations for training and performed well in many competitions. It was renamed the 4th battalion of the 11th Sikh regiment in the 1922 reforms. In WW II, the battalion moved to Egypt where it fought against Italian and German forces. From there, it was sent to Italy, where it was deployed in the Gothic Lines fighting against both German and Italian forces. The battalion stayed in Italy after the world war was over until 1946.

After Independence, the battalion was renamed the 4th battalion of the Sikh Regiment. Later, the battalion got the chance to prove its mettle again in Walong in the 1962 Indo-China War. China used waves after waves of their army to capture the area but here also, just like Saragarhi, determined men with the blessings of the martyrs fought until the last round. A sepoy in the unit named Kewal Singh showed mettle similar to the bravado of the Saragarhi warriors when he dashed out of his bunker after his ammunition ran out, and fought and killed eight enemies singlehandedly with a bayonet and his bare hands. He was awarded the Mahavir Chakra for this act of valour. After an intense battle that spanned 25 days, the battalion was told to retreat, to the utter dismay of officers and men.

The next opportunity to fight was bestowed upon the battalion in Pakistan. It was 7 September 1965 when the unit received orders to advance to Lahore, clearing all oppositions en route along the Khalra–Lahore road. It started with the capture of a few border outposts. On 8 September, the unit was told to advance for the town of Barki and the Ichhogil Canal Bridge. Barki was heavily fortified by pill boxes and anti tank guns. The attack started at 20.00 hrs on 10 September and Barki was captured by 21.30 hrs. Here, again, the battalion earned its name as, in another brave act, Subedar Ajit Singh was assigned to destroy a gun emplacement of the enemy which he did singlehandedly despite being hit by a burst of bullets by the gun emplacement. He was awarded the Mahavir Chakra posthumously for his bravery and courage.

In 1971, the battalion was in the Eastern Front and was ordered to capture Siramani. However, before that could happen, it had to capture three other villages – Makapur, Chaugacha and Burinda. At the end, the battalion was awarded three Vir Chakras and the battle honour of Siramani. In fact, the battalion is also credited with the shooting down of a Pakistan Air Force Sabre by an LMG. The enemy pilot ejected and was captured, only to be released later. That pilot, Flight Lieutenant Pervez Mehdi, went on to become the 8th Chief of Air Staff of the Pakistan Air Force.

India has not been at full-fledged war since 1971 but 4 Sikh (36th) has still remained at the top and has continued to honour those brave 21 – a tradition that had started on 12 September 1897. In fact, during the battalion's United Nations tenure it was deployed in Lebanon, and despite the continuous disturbances in the area and advice of hierarchy to move out, the battalion did not back down an inch. It not only stayed true to its moral code but also to the UN Peacekeeping Forces'. It was awarded UNFIL citation for its bravery.

Be it any time or any circumstance, the stand taken in Saragarhi will always be in the hearts of the unit's soldiers, and will continue to be so for its future legatees as well. Being in the unit and reading its history, it is amply clear to me as a young officer that it was my luck to have been commissioned in the 36th and I shall forever strive to live up to the standards set by the battalion.

'Bole so nihaal, sat shri akal!'

Appendix

The following details the force level of the Tirah Campaign, commanded by General Sir William Stephen Alexander Lockhart. K.C.B, K.C.S.I.

First Division, *commanded by Brigadier-General William Penn Symons, C.B.*

First Brigade, *commanded by Brigadier-General R. C. Hart, V.C., C.B.*
2nd Battalion The Derbyshire Regiment
1st Battalion The Devonshire Regiment
2nd/1st Gurkha (Rifle) Regiment
30th (Punjab) Regiment of Bengal Infantry
No. 6 British Field Hospital
No 34 Native Field Hospital

Second Brigade, *commanded by Brigadier-General A. Gaselee, C.B.*
2nd Battalion The Yorkshire Regiment
1st Battalion Royal West Surrey Regiment

2nd Battalion 4th Gurkha (Rifle) Regiment
3rd Regiment of Sikh Infantry, Punjab Frontier Force
Sections A and B of No. 8 British Field Hospital
Sections A and C of No. 14 British Field Hospital
No. 51 Native Hospital

Divisional Troops (First Division)
No. 1 Mountain Battery, Royal Artillery
No. 2 (Derajat) Mountain Battery
No. 1 (Kohat) Mountain Battery
Two Squadrons, 18th Regiment of Bengal Lancers
28th Regiment of Bombay Infantry (Pioneers)
No. 3 Company, Bombay Sappers and Miners
No. 4 Company, Bombay Sappers and Miners
One Printing Section from the Bombay Sappers and
Miners
The Nabha Regiment of Imperial Service Infantry
The Maler Kotla Imperial Service Sappers
Section A of No. 13 British Field Hospital
No. 63 Native Field Hospital

Second Division, *commanded by Major General A.G.*
Yeatman-Biggs, C.B.

Third Brigade, *commanded by Colonel F.J. Kempster,*
D.S.O, A.D.C.
1st Battalion The Gordon Highlanders
1st Battalion The Dorsetshire Regiment

1st Battalion 2nd Gurkha (Rifle) Regiment
15th (The Ludhiana Sikh) Regiment of Bengal
Infantry
No. 24 British Field Hospital
No. 44 Native Field Hospital

Fourth Brigade, *commanded by Brigadier-General R. Westmacott, C.B, D.S.O.*
2nd Battalion The King's own Scottish Borderers
1st Battalion The Northamptonshire Regiment
1st Battalion 3rd Gurkha (Rifle) Regiment
36th (Sikh) Regiment of Bengal Infantry
Sections C and D of No. 9 Field Hospital
Sections A and B of No. 23 British Field Hospital
No. 48 Native Field Hospital

Divisional Troops
No. 8 Mountain Battery, Royal Artillery
No. 9 Mountain Battery, Royal Artillery
No. 5 (Bombay) Mountain Battery
Machine Gun Detachment, 16th Lancers
Two Squadrons 18th Regiment of Bengal Lancers
21st Regiment of Madras Infantry (Pioneers)
No. 4 Company, Madras Sappers And Miners
One Printing Section from The Madras Sappers and
Miners
The Jhind Regiment of Imperial Service Infantry
The Sirmur Imperial Service Sappers

Section B of No. 13 British Field Hospital
No. 43 Native Field Hospital

Line of Communications, *commanded by Lieutenant-General Sir A.P. Palmer, K.C.B.*
No. 1 Kashmir Mountain Battery
22nd (Punjab) Regiment of Bengal Infantry
2nd Battalion, 2nd Gurkha (Rifle) Regiment
39th (Gurhwal Rifle) Regiment of Bengal Infantry
2nd Regiment of Punjab Infantry, Punjab Frontier Force
3rd Regiment of Bengal Cavalry
18th Regiment, Bengal Lancers
No. 1 Company, Bengal Sappers and Miners
No. 42 Native Field Hospital
No. 52 Native Field Hospital
The Jeypore Imperial Service Transport Corps
The Gwalior Imperial Service Transport Corps
Ordnance Field Park
Engineer Field Park
British General Hospital, of 500 beds, at Rawalpindi
Native General Hospital, of 500 beds, at Rawalpindi
No. 1 Field Medical Store Depot
No. 2 Field Medical Store Depot
No. 5 Veterinary Field Hospital
No. 11 British Field Hospital
No. 25 British Field Hospital
No. 47 Native Field Hospital
No. 64 Native Field Hospital

The Peshawar Column, *commanded by Brigadier-General A.G. Hammond, C.B, D.S.O, V.C, A.D.C.*
2nd Battalion, The Royal Inniskilling Fusiliers
2nd Battalion, The Oxfordshire Light Infantry
9th Gurkha (Rifle) Regiment of Bengal Infantry
34th Pioneers
45th (Rattray's Sikh) Regiment of Bengal Infantry
57th Field Battery, Royal Artillery
No. 3 Mountain Battery, Royal Artillery
9th Regiment of Bengal Lancers
No. 5 Company, Bengal Sappers and Miners
No. 5 British Field Hospital
No. 45 Native Field Hospital, A and B Sections
British General Hospital, of 250 beds, at Nowshera
Native General Hospital, of 500 beds, at Nowshera

The Kurram Movable Column, *commanded by Colonel W. Hill, Indian Staff Corps*
12th (Khelat-i-Ghilzai) Regiment of Bengal Infantry
1st Battalion, 5th Gurkha Rifles
The Kapurthala Regiment of Imperial Service Infantry
3rd Field Battery, Royal Artillery
6th Regiment of Bengal Cavalry
One Regiment of Central India Horse
Section D of No. 3 British Field Hospital
No. 62 Native Field Hospital
Section B of No. 46 Native Field Hospital
Native General Hospital, of 200 beds, at Kohat

The Rawalpindi Reserve Brigade, *commanded by Brigadier-General C.R. MacGregor, D.S.O.*
2nd Battalion, The King's Own Yorkshire Light Infantry
1st Battalion, The Duke of Cornwall's Light Infantry
27th Regiment (1st Baluch Battalion) of Bombay (Light) Infantry
2nd Regiment of Infantry, Hyderabad Contingent
Jodhpur Imperial Service Lancers
No. 12 British Field Hospital
No. 53 Native Field Hospital

Acknowledgements

Nirvan Singh

I find this part of a book hard to write but for once, I did not have to labour much. Ever since I was a child, I wanted to study the service records of Indian soldiers particularly in the colonial era, probably because I had grown up listening to stories of my great grandfather, Lance Naik Phangan Singh, and his heroics in WW1 for which he was conferred with an Indian Order of Merit by the British. Amidst the countless episodes of unmatched bravery of Indian troops that I came across, the Battle of Saragarhi in particular caught my attention. As a consequence, I started to collect facts and data on the heroic stand taken by the 21 gallant Sikh soldiers against 10,000 Afghan tribesmen. To write a book on the battle, however, was a whole different task altogether.

At the outset, I express my gratitude to Suhail Mathur of the Book Bakers Literary Agency. When one is blessed with a literary agent as adamant and visionary as Suhail, one goes on to do the least expected things in the most unexpected ways. 'Write it and finish it in the given time, and do not worry, I am there,' was his reply to my 'I don't think we can do it'. This was, however, only half the push required; the other half came from my co-author, Kirandeep Singh, an extremely artistic and learned man whose energy to work on this subject was even greater than mine. Together, we form a team and I cannot thank him enough for leading this team responsibly towards its objective.

I also express my gratitude to our publishers, Bloomsbury India, and our editor Prerna Vohra for believing in us and giving us an opportunity to present the story of this saga to the world.

The credit for the very first kickstart required for this book goes to Kuldeep sir and the entire team of officers of 4 Sikh (erstwhile 36th Sikhs). One evening, over a cup of coffee, I remember having questioned Kuldeep sir about the meaning of a Punjabi song he would sing at occasions: '*Beri naal ne ber hunde, aive ta nai kisse ban'de, asi sachi haan sher hunde* (Legends they say about us aren't untrue for we truly belong to the race of lions).' He stated that '4 Sikh' was the proud legatee of the 36th Sikhs and they were the successors of the brave 21 soldiers of the Saragarhi saga. This was when I realized I could ask him and his unit to help me with the research for this book and, humble as he is, he agreed at once. Also, I would like to thank

Rahul Harmon Sir for introducing me to Kuldeep sir. The battalion's consistent help throughout the research would not have been possible without the consent of their Commanding Officer, so I thank Colonel S.K. (full name withheld) for his quick response to all our requests. My access to the information we required was through the young and vibrant officer RR (name withheld for privacy reasons) who was always available even at odd hours of the night. You were tolerant, my friend.

I take this opportunity to extend my heartiest gratitude to Lieutenant General S.K. Jha, PVSM, AVSM, YSM, SM, Colonel of the Sikh Regiment, whose motivating message for this book powered me to deliver my best to live up to the expected standards.

The story of the Battle of Saragarhi has been made into a period drama motion picture named *Kesari*, starring Akshay Kumar and directed by Anurag Singh, who was humble enough to compliment us for our book on the subject. I thank him profoundly for the same.

The list of those who contributed to the compilation, collation and writing of this book – or who, at some point in time, have supported me in my endeavours – is long but I do not intend to miss even one name. To that end, I would like to express my gratitude to Vasu Sir, Y.K. Singh sir, Saikat Sarkar sir, Sanjeev Dewan sir, Pankaj Sir, Geetika ma'am, Arnavaz ma'am, Shweta ma'am, Bhaavna Arora ma'am, Vishal Thapa sir, Aditya sir, Arun sir, Jaiman sir, Hemant sir, Chirag sir, Ravi sir,

Amandeep sir, Goregaonkar A.P. sir; my course mates Akshay Tikkar, Mohit Kadyan, Kolli Sudheer, Gauravjit, Ashutosh, Shaleen, Ankur Agnihotri, Nirmala, Pupinder, Shivam; my friends and cousins, Sajan, Suraj, Pranav, Ashish, Ravish, Harpreet, Rajwinder, Parth, Mohit, Nitin, Tanya, Sushim, Arpit, Sakshi Koul, Baljeet Singh Maan, Kuljeet Singh Maan, Harminderjit, Rohan; my *mama ji*(s), Parshotam Mahajan, Pawan Gupta, Chander Mahajan Sukesh Mahajan, Yash Mahajan; my sister, Kimi; my love and my personal critic, Aarushi; and my stress-relieving fur-babies Scooby and Sultan.

Perseverance and passion are inherent qualities passed on to me by my parents and my grandmother and I can never thank them enough for all that they have done for me. To them, I owe everything.

Lastly, I thank *Waheguru* for protecting me and making me capable enough to follow my passions in life.

Kirandeep Singh Phul

I would like to begin by stating that I feel honoured to have been given this opportunity to put the heroic saga of the 21 bravehearts of Saragarhi into words. I could not have worked on this book without the help of my co-author, Nirvan Singh, an extraordinary human being. I am grateful to Suhail Mathur of the Book Bakers Literary Agency for putting his faith in us, and to BIoomsbury for once again giving us an opportunity to publish a book with them after *Nasteya: The Aryan Saga*, which was released in December 2018. I thank Prerna Vohra for going through the arduous task of editing our book, and doing it outstandingly. Further, I am indebted to my grandfather Dr Gurdial Singh Phul and my parents, S. Rabinder Singh Phul and Ramjit Kaur, for instilling storytelling skills in me. These skills are polished daily by my son, Pavitdeep Singh, who doesn't sleep without a new bedtime story every night. I hope for this phenomenon to continue even as he grows up.

Whenever a writer formulates a new plot, he needs someone who would listen to it and assess it and, thankfully, my wife, Jiwan Jyoti; my friends, Vikas Mittal, Tejinder Pal Singh (JP), Ranjit Singh, Gursahib Singh, Bhupinder Singh, Simranjit Walia, Dr Narender Sharma; and my elder brother S. Amandeep Singh Phul served as my soundboards.

We could not have come this far without the invaluable support of Harbir Singh, Nakul Malik, Professor S.K. Arora, Professor Charanjit Singh, Irwanpreet Singh and Neha Sharma, and I thank all of them profusely for their help. I would also like to thank S. Jaspal Singh and Dr Sangeet Phul, S. Satpal Singh and Jasbir Kaur, along with the whole Mattewal family for always tolerating me while I wrote and hosting my untimely meals as and when needed.

Lastly, I express my thanks to Dr Akashdeep Singh Chandi, Vice Chairman at Global Institutes, Amritsar, for always supporting us and answering all our queries. I am also grateful to Dr Manish Bansal, Dr Iqbal Singh and all my teachers at MIMIT, Malout and my confidante Rabia Arora for kindling the flame of writing in me.

Lastly, here's a message for my constant companion for the last eleven years: 'Dear Shaggy, your presence in my study room, in my house and in my life will always be missed. You may be gone, but I sense you around me, my furry friend.'

About the Authors

Kiran Nirvan is the pseudonym used by authors Kirandeep Singh and Nirvan Singh.

Kirandeep Singh is the co-author of the bestselling book *Nasteya: The Aryan Saga*. He is the former head of the Department of Management Studies, Global Institutes, Amritsar, and is currently pursuing his doctorate in the discipline. Kirandeep began exploring his passion for writing in his teenage years and has authored more than a hundred poems in Punjabi.

Nirvan Singh is a serving officer in the Indian army, while also being an artist, writer and adventurer. The Battle of Saragarhi is one of the stories that inspired him to follow in his father's footsteps and join the armed forces.